Vatican II:
The Catholic Challenge

VATICAN II:
The Catholic Challenge

Why Just "Being Catholic"
Isn't Enough Anymore

ALAN SCHRECK

CHARIS
Servant Publications
Ann Arbor, Michigan

Charis Books is an imprint of Servant Publications especially designed to serve Roman Catholics.

The Scripture quotations contained herein are from the Revised Standard Version Bible, Catholic Edition, copyright 1965 and 1966 by the Division of Christian Education of the National Council of the Churches of Christ in USA, and are used by permission.

Quotations from documents of the Second Vatican Council are reprinted with permission of America Press, Inc., 106 W. 56th Street, New York, New York 10019. Copyright 1966. All rights reserved.

Published by Servant Publications
P.O. Box 8617
Ann Arbor, Michigan 48107

Cover design by Diane Bareis

Printed in the United States of America
ISBN 0-89283-684-9

94 95 10 9 8 7 6 5 4 3

Nihil obstat   Monsignor Joseph P. Malara
                Censor Librorum
Imprimatur: Most Reverend Albert H. Ottenweller
             Bishop of Steubenville

The *nihil obstat* and *imprimatur* are official declarations that a book or pamphlet is free from doctrinal or moral error. No implication is contained therein that those who grant the *nihil obstat* or *imprimatur* agree with the contents, opinions, or statements expressed.

Contents

ACKNOWLEDGMENTS

I WOULD LIKE TO GRATEFULLY ACKNOWLEDGE the support of the Franciscan University of Steubenville for providing a research grant which made it possible for me to begin research on this book, as well as providing me with over ten years' of teaching experience on the graduate level on the subject of this book. I thank my students over those years who have deepened my love and sharpened my understanding of the Second Vatican Council.

Special thanks are due to Mrs. Norma Donohue for her tireless secretarial work; to Roger Lemire for special research; to David Came of Servant Publications for editorial assistance; and to my wife, Nancy, my family, and friends for their encouragement and steadfast prayers.

Note to the Reader

THERE ARE SOME VERY GOOD ENGLISH translations of the documents of the Second Vatican Council, which were originally written in Latin. The author has chosen to quote from *The Documents of Vatican II*, Walter M. Abbott, S.J., general editor, and the Very Rev. Msgr. Joseph Gallagher, translation editor. This choice was based on the general readibility of the text for the popular reader. However, the author has found some other editions, such as the Austin Flannery, O.P. edition, more accurate in the translation of some passages.

References throughout the text proper refer to the standard chapter and section numbers used by all versions of the documents, so that this book may be used in conjunction with any translation or edition preferred by the reader. However, in the recommended reading sections which appear at the end of each chapter, references are made by page number to the Abbott and Flannery editions.

Here is the pertinent publishing information for the Abbott and Flannery editions. The Abbott edition is copyright © 1966 by the American Press and is now published by Association Press, New Century Publishers, Inc. The address is: 220 New Brunswick Road, Piscataway, New Jersey, 08854. The Flannery edition is copyright © 1975 by Costello Publishing Company, Inc., and Reverend Austin Flannery, O.P. It is published by William B. Eerdmans Publishing Company. The address is: 255 Jefferson Avenue S.E., Grand Rapids, Michigan, 49503.

Abbreviations for Church Documents

1. Abbreviations of Council Documents:

AA *Decree on the Apostolate of the Laity,*
Apostolicam actuositatem

AG *Decree on the Missionary Activity of the Church,*
Ad gentes

CD *Decree on the Pastoral Office of Bishops in the Church,*
Christus Dominus

DH *Declaration on Religious Freedom,*
Dignitatis humanae

DV *Dogmatic Constitution on Divine Revelation,*
Dei Verbum

GE ***Declaration on Christian Education,***
Gravissimum educationis

GS *Pastoral Constitution on the Church in the Modern World,*
Gaudium et spes

IM *Decree on the Means of Social Communication,*
Inter mirifica

LG *Dogmatic Constitution on the Church,*
Lumen gentium

NA *Declaration on the Relation of the Church to Non-Christian Religions,* ***Nostra aetate***

OE *Decree on the Catholic Eastern Churches,*
Orientalium Ecclesiarum

OT *Decree on the Priestly Formation,*
Optatum totius

PC *Decree on the Up-to-Date Renewal of Religious Life,*
Perfectae caritatis

PO *Decree on the Ministry and Life of Priests,*
Presbyterorum ordinis

SC *Constitution on the Sacred Liturgy,*
Sacrosanctum concilium

UR *Decree on Ecumenism,*
Unitatis redintegratio

2. Abbreviations of Other Documents:

CL *The Lay Members of Christ's Faithful People,*
Pope John Paul II, Dec. 30, 1988,
Christifideles Laici

DC *On the Mystery and Worship of the Eucharist,*
Pope John Paul II, February 24, 1980,
Dominicae Cenae

LE *On Human Work, Pope John Paul II, September 14, 1981,*
Laborem Exercens

ES *Extraordinary Synod, 1985*

VQ *On the 25th Anniversary of the Constitution on*
the Sacred Liturgy, Pope John Paul II, December 4, 1988,
Vicesimus quintus

Introduction

IT IS A CURIOUS FACT that the Catholic church remains the largest united Christian body, yet its teaching and mission appear shrouded in mystery to the eyes of much of the world, even to many Catholics. How often does one hear questions like the following raised by Protestants and Catholics alike:

- Are Catholics encouraged to read the Bible, and do they really believe that it is the Word of God? How do Catholics interpret the Bible?
- What are the roles of "Tradition" and the teaching office of the pope and the bishops in deciding Catholic beliefs? Are they more important than the teachings of the Bible itself?
- What role do lay people, especially women, play in the life and ministry of the Catholic church today? Have the roles of bishops, priests, and religious brothers and sisters changed from times past? What is the basis for the authority of the pope and the Vatican in guiding the church?
- Is the Catholic church really interested in promoting Christian unity? Does the Catholic church recognize Protestant and Orthodox believers as fellow Christians?
- Does the Catholic church still have a mission to convert non-Christians? Can Catholics blend beliefs or practices from non-Christian religions into their faith?
- What is the point of the church's involvement in things like politics, science, and culture? Is it really appropriate for the church to take a leading role in the affairs of the world?

As we consider these questions and our response to them, we are presented simultaneously with a great opportunity and an immense challenge. Perhaps Richard John Neuhaus has expressed it best in our time. In 1987, Neuhaus (then a Lutheran pastor and now a Roman Catholic) published a widely read book, *The Catholic Moment*. He argued that the Catholic church was in the best position to lead Christians in advancing the cause of Christ in the world today.

However, Neuhaus noted that there was no guarantee that the Catholic church would grasp "the Catholic Moment" and succeed in assuming the reins of leadership. That would depend upon the responsiveness of Catholics to God's call—especially their heeding of the prophetic direction being set by key Catholic leaders, such as Pope John Paul II and Cardinal Joseph Ratzinger.

Though certain points of Neuhaus' book have been debated, I certainly agree with him about the unique position of the Catholic church in Christianity and in the world. I believe the Jesus Christ founded the Catholic church and has gifted it with the fullness of the means of grace and salvation. I also agree with Neuhaus, though, that the Catholic church in each age *can* fail to take the lead in Christian life and world mission. This may happen in our own age if Catholics fail to follow the guidance which God is providing and do not respond to his grace, which is abundantly available through the Catholic church.

Thus "the Catholic Moment" becomes supremely "the Catholic Challenge." Seeking to address that challenge in our age will be the central aim of this book. I will address the special call and guidance that God is giving to the Catholic church in our time, so that she might be an inspiration and source of hope for other Christians, as well as a "light to the nations," leading all people to the fullness of life and truth in Jesus Christ.

What exactly is the unique challenge that God is giving to the Catholic church today? Certainly, I believe that this call is being presented through our current church leaders, such as John Paul II, Mother Teresa of Calcutta, and Cardinal Ratzinger, among many others. But if we look back a bit, we find that much of their work and teaching is based upon a monumental event that has shaped our understanding of the life and mission of the Catholic church today. This great event is the Second Vatican Council, whose final session was held twenty-five years ago at this writing.

The challenge of Vatican II for Catholics today

Vatican II: The Catholic Challenge focuses primarily on the challenge and call that God has given to Catholics through the Second Vatican Council. This book is based on the strong belief that the teaching of Vatican II remains a primary guide, if not the primary guide, for Catholics in the 1990s and into the next century, precisely because so many of its challenges have yet to be fulfilled or even heeded.

There is a temptation to believe that the teachings of Vatican II are no longer relevant, having been eclipsed by new agendas and issues. Although some things have changed, I think that we will discover in the pages of this book that most of the Council's teachings are surprisingly relevant today.

But do we even know what Vatican II *really* teaches? Historian James Hitchcock observed several years ago that the decrees of Vatican II "...remain among the most unread documents of modern times. Although practically everyone, Catholic and non-Catholic, has an impression of what the Council said and did, relatively few demonstrate an intimate familiarity with its actual statements."[1] The sad fact is that many Catholics simply have not read the documents of Vatican II, so they are prey to vague impressions or inaccurate interpretations of the Council's teaching. Even Catholic theologians have been known to censor or distort passages of the Council documents.

For instance, how often have Catholics heard about the "spirit" of Vatican II, without knowing whether this "spirit" accurately reflects what the Council actually taught? Or when we hear that the Council was primarily pastoral, does this mean that it does not teach doctrine?

In response to such questions, in 1985, Pope John Paul II called an Extraordinary Synod of Bishops from around the world to discuss the true meaning of Vatican II and to evaluate the results to date. The Synod reaffirmed, "The message of Vatican proposes to us for our time, 'the inexhaustible riches of the mystery of Christ...'" (ES, p.30).

While acknowledging that abundant fruit has been borne by the Council, the bishops at the Extraordinary Synod also recognized many traumatic problems, especially in the West. These include a mass exodus from the priesthood and religious life, declining numbers of Catholics attending Sunday Mass and the sacrament of reconciliation, and the shocking increase of the divorce rate among Catholics.

Although many current difficulties in the church are unrelated to the Council itself, real problems have arisen from ignorance or misinterpretation of the full teaching of the Council—even failure to implement its true doctrine. To remedy this, the Extraordinary Synod called for a fresh study and teaching of the message of the Second Vatican Council through both scholarly and popular presentations (ES, p. 42).

I have tried to respond to that call by writing this book. My intent is to take a fresh look at the teachings of Vatican II and to bring the Council's authentic message to Catholics today. To this end, *Vatican II: The Catholic Challenge* will highlight in particular the *challenge* of believing and practicing the faith. It will explain why just "being Catholic" isn't enough anymore. We must understand and live the faith in its fullness.

How to use this book

Certainly, this book should not be substituted for reading the documents of Vatican II. It should be viewed primarily as an introductory guide to the documents, which hopefully will entice readers to explore the Council's work themselves.

Vatican II: The Catholic Challenge contains frequent references to the Council documents and other church documents. These are placed parenthetically in the text, using the abbreviations listed at the beginning of the book. The numbers in these parenthetical references indicate the standard paragraph numbers in the text. They do not refer to chapter or page numbers. Parenthetical references to the Extraordinary Synod of 1985 (ES) are the sole exception of this in the text proper; they refer to page numbers in a book published by the Daughters of St. Paul (*Extraordinary Synod—1985* [Boston, MA: St. Paul Books & Media],1986).

Both individuals and groups are encouraged to use the practical application sections at the end of each chapter. These sections provide:

1. Recommended readings in the document or documents studied in the chapter, with page references to the two most frequently use English translations of the Vatican II documents;
2. Questions for discussion for use by groups, such as those in adult religious education programs in parishes or college and university courses covering Vatican II;
3. A personal challenge to help the individual reader apply the particular teaching covered in the chapter to his or her life;
4. A resource list for further study.

Groups should not feel obligated to answer all of the questions for discussion in these practical application sections. Rather, group leaders should select the questions that seem most helpful, given the needs and time constraints of their particular group. Further, individuals will need to decide whether to commit themselves to following through on the personal challenges. If you decide to tackle the personal challenges, select only one at a time. Remember that any significant change in attitude or behavior takes at least several weeks of diligent effort before taking hold as a habit. Normally, you should not expect immediate results.

In fact, throughout this book, we will explore many challenges posed to Catholics by the Council—both in the practical application sections and throughout the text proper. As a result, some readers may begin to feel overwhelmed by the sheer number of challenges, not knowing where to begin or how to respond.

I believe it is important to remember two things in responding to these challenges. First, the Lord expects each person to take up only one small part of the challenges he is presenting to the entire church. We need to remember that we belong to the body of Christ. Since the body has many members, each member need do only the particular work that God assigns, not more.

Second, how do each of us determine what God is calling us to do in response to these challenges? We should pray that God will show us how we are meant to respond. This discernment of God's will may also be aided by a trusted pastor, or Catholic friend. In prayer and through discernment about our own situation, God will show each of us how to respond.

How much authority do the teachings of Vatican II have?

Some people have raised the question of the level of authority of the Council's teachings. After all, *if* the Council documents are not authoritative and groundbreaking in some way, why should we make the effort to study them? I would make the following observations on this question.

First, the form of the Council's teaching is important to note. Nowhere in the documents of Vatican II do we find formal doctrinal definitions or "canons" that precisely define articles of faith. Some of the documents are definitely more concerned with providing pastoral guidelines and direction for church life, rather than formally presenting articles of faith.

Does this mean that Vatican II teaches no doctrine that Catholics are bound to believe? Certainly not!

Ecumenical (meaning worldwide) Councils of the church are solemn events in which all of the Catholic bishops of the world are invited to discuss and vote on issues that affect the entire church. Catholics understand that such Councils are guided by the Holy Spirit in a special way. Thus official teachings of these Councils have great authority—even when they are not presented as formal definitions of faith.

In fact, at the Second Vatican Council, the four documents entitled "constitutions" are particularly important. The Extraordinary Synod of 1985 states, "Special attention should be paid to the four major constitutions of the Council, which contain the interpretative key for the other decrees and declarations" (ES, p. 41).

Further, the teachings of Vatican II present in contemporary terms and language many truths and doctrines that have long been believed and officially taught by the Catholic church. Vatican II neither simply repeats past doctrinal understandings, nor does it present truths that can be isolated from past teachings of the Catholic church. The Extraordinary Synod explains, "The Council must be understood in continuity with the great tradition of the Church, and at the same time, we must receive light from the Council's own doctrine for today's Church and the people of our time. The Church is one and the same throughout all the Councils: "(ES, p. 41).

This means that Catholics are not free to discount all past teachings or Councils of the Catholic church, as if Vatican II has replaced or superseded them. Nor may Catholics ignore or minimize the importance of the teaching of the Second Vatican Council in areas in which the Council deepens, extends, or puts into fresh language the Catholic understanding of Christianity.

Vatican II does challenge us to accept some new and deeper understandings of our Catholic Christian faith! For instance, as we shall see in chapter 1, *The Dogmatic Constitution on Divine Revelation* presents an extremely helpful and deeper understanding of the Bible and "Tradition" with a capital "T" as the one Word of God, showing the close connection between the two.

The challenge of Vatican II, as described here, might be best expressed in the words of the many whom God inspired to call the Council: Pope John XXIII. In his speech convoking the Council, John XXIII expressed the balance between the "new things and the old" (cf. Mt 13:52) which the Lord, as the faithful householder, wished to bring forth from the Second Vatican Council. He noted that the greatest concern of the Council was that the sacred deposit of Christian doctrine be handed on faithfully and taught more effectively to our age. The church must simultaneously remain faithful to the past and "never depart from the sacred patrimony received from the Fathers. But at the same time, she must ever look to the present, to the new conditions and new forms of life introduced into the modern world, which have opened up new avenues to the Catholic apostolate...."

Pope John XXIII emphasized that is was not necessary to call a Council simply to repeat the church's fundamental doctrine in a way that was already familiar to everyone. The church and the world needed a deeper understanding and a renewed expression of its doctrine. The reasoning behind this is expressed aptly in this crucial sentence of his speech, "The substance of the ancient doctrine is one thing, and the way in which it is presented is another."

Because the approach of the Council was to be predominantly pastoral—to open avenues of understanding and renewal within the church and between the church and the world—there would be no condemnations or formal definitions offered by the Second Vatican Council. Rather it would seek to express the faith of the Catholic church in a way that Catholics and others in our time could understand and accept.[2]

But will we accept the invitation of the bishops at the Extraordinary Synod to know more fully the work of the Second Vatican Council and put its teachings more deeply into practice? "The message of Vatican II, like that of the Councils which have marked the history of the Church, cannot bring forth its fruits except through a sustained and persevering effort" (EX, p.32).

Let us decide now to take a fresh look at the message of Vatican II, with the realization that just "being Catholic" isn't enough anymore. We need to live our faith in the full sense of the word. Should anyone be surprised that the teachings of the Second Vatican Council are as demanding and challenging as the teaching of Jesus himself? We certainly shouldn't be surprised since the goal of Vatican II is to apply the gospel of Jesus Christ to our times.

A merely cultural or nominal approach to Catholicism will not sustain our faith—especially in our age of secularism. Instead, we must accept the Catholic challenge by fully understanding and then living our faith in the 1990s and into the twenty-first century.

ONE

Knowing and Living God's Word

How do you respond when you notice a clean-cut representative of another religious body, like the Jehovah's Witnesses, approaching your front door? Are you confident that you will be able to explain your faith and its biblical basis in a simple and convincing way? Sadly, many Catholics are unable to do so because they don't understand how their Catholic faith is rooted in God's Word as it comes to us in sacred Scripture, sacred Tradition, and through the teaching office of the church.

A colleague of mine who became a Catholic after years as a convinced Presbyterian and a pastor in that church said that he was stunned to discover, when he began to investigate the Catholic faith, that Catholics actually revere the Bible as the Word of God. Further, he was surprised to discover that Catholics draw their basic beliefs, including beliefs about Tradition and the church's magisterium, from the Bible.

To me it is ironic that while informed Catholics are ready to point out that the Bible is "our book," the "book of the church," relatively few Catholics read and study the Bible regularly. Relatively few know what "our book" teaches as well as many other Christians do. Hence, the challenge to

Catholics today in this area is two-fold. First, we must *know the Word of God,* so that we will "always be prepared to make a defense to anyone who calls you to account for the hope that is in you, . . . with gentleness and reverence" (1 Pt 3:15). Second, Catholics must *live the Word of God* by putting it into practice. Our salvation depends on being "doers of the word, and not hearers only, deceiving [ourselves]" (Jas 1:22). These two challenges, of course, are related because we cannot live God's word unless we understand it and know what it really means.

The Second Vatican Council addresses the questions of what God's Word is and how it comes to us. The Council invites us to put the Word into practice in our daily lives. It is not surprising then that one of the four primary documents of Vatican II, called "constitutions," is *The Dogmatic Constitution on Divine Revelation.* The Latin title is simply **Dei Verbum** (**DV**): The Word of God.

Let's examine what this document has to say as it addresses some important questions often asked about God's revelation.

Why do we need God's Word?

This document stresses that the main purpose of God's revelation is not to deliver commands from on high, nor is it to provide important information about God or about the universe. God has chosen to reveal himself to the human race in order to invite us into a personal relationship of friendship and fellowship with himself (**DV**, no. 2).

What a tremendous offer! Out of God's pure, unmerited love, he desires to share his life with us and to make us his friends and even members of his family. God reveals himself that we might accept his invitation to life, thus becoming daughters and sons of God, and brothers and sisters of the Son of God who became man, Jesus Christ.

We can come to know of God's existence indirectly

through nature or creation. But as God reveals himself through the Jewish and Christian Scriptures, he can be known "with ease, with solid certitude, and with no trace of error, ..." (**DV**, no. 6).

What God reveals about himself is life-giving and life-changing. The Old Testament teaches that "man does not live by bread alone, but ... by everything that proceeds out of the mouth of the LORD" (Dt 8:3). The New Testament records Jesus' teaching: "the words I have spoken to you are spirit and life" (Jn 6:63). Jesus promises his followers "If you continue in my word, you are truly my disciples, and you will know the truth, and the truth will make you free" (Jn 8:31-32).

In God's Word we find truth, freedom, and life. Why settle for anything less?

Is there any new revelation?

Jesus Christ, who is God's eternal Word made flesh, is the final and fullest revelation to humanity of God's own nature and identity. In Jesus, God has made with us a "new and definitive covenant, [which] will never pass away, and we now await no further new public revelation before the glorious manifestation [the Second Coming] of our Lord Jesus Christ (cf. 1 Tm 6:14 and Ti 2:13)" (**DV**, no. 4).

Jesus is the climax of God's revelation of himself—because he is the very image of the Father (Col 1:15), in whom all the fullness of God was pleased to dwell. This is why Catholics cannot accept non-Christian religions as revelations of God equal to that found in Christ. God's revelation of himself in Jesus Christ is unsurpassed and unsurpassable. Therefore Catholics reject additions to Christianity, such as by Mormons or the New Age movement, that clearly have no root or basis in the public revelation of Christ in the first century. The Catholic church, along with many other Christian traditions, believes that this privileged period of public revelation ended with the death of the last apostle of Jesus.

What is our response to God's revelation?

God has totally given himself and revealed himself to us in Jesus Christ. The only fitting response on our part is to believe fully in his revelation and to give ourselves totally to God. As the constitution states: "'The obedience of faith' (Rom 16:26; cf. 1:5; 2 Cor 10:5-6) must be given to God who reveals, an obedience by which man entrusts his whole self freely to God, . . . and freely assenting to the truth revealed by Him" (no. 5).

As Jesus promised, when we come to believe in him, "we will know the truth and the truth will make us free" (Jn 8:32). In obedience to God, humanity discovers true freedom.

How does the Bible come to us?

God revealed himself to the ancient Hebrew people and later came among us in fullness in Jesus Christ. It is reasonable to ask how we can know with certainty what actually happened thousands of years ago. Catholics believe that all the writings found in the Old and New Testament are written under the inspiration of the Holy Spirit and hence have God as their author. The writers of the sacred Sripture, though, are also true authors of the Bible. God used their human talents and abilities, along with their limited cultural backgrounds, to communicate those truths he wanted written down (DV, no. 11). The Bible is truly "the Word of God in the words of man."

We have this unique set of writings comprising the Bible preserved two thousand to three thousand years after their composition, because they have been safeguarded and handed on to us by the Hebrew people of the old covenant, and by the church of the new covenant founded by Jesus Christ.

We can outline the steps by which the New Testament has come down to us (see DV, nos. 7 and 8).

1. Christ commissioned the apostles to preach to all people. They faithfully handed on, by word of mouth and example, all that they had received from Christ himself or learned through the prompting of the Holy Spirit.

2. Apostles and those who worked with them wrote down this revelation, under the inspiration of the Holy Spirit. Letters of the apostles and various Gospels, which are orderly collections of the oral and written teaching about Jesus (see Lk 1), were circulated among the local communities of the early church.

3. The apostles left bishops as their successors. They were "handing over their own teaching role to them" (St. Irenaeus, c. A.D. 185), so that the truth handed on to them, whether in the apostolic preaching or in inspired writings, would be preserved until the end of time.

4. The bishops of the early church developed official lists ("canons") of inspired writings. They believed these writings expressed God's revelation most fully and faithfully. Although slightly different canons emerged in the early church, by the Middle Ages a consensus had been reached that the forty-six writings of the Old Testament and the twenty-seven writings of New Testament that comprise the present "Catholic Bible" were all inspired by the Holy Spirit and are God's revelation for all time.

Is the Bible alone God's Word?

The Bible is God's Word, but Catholics do not believe that God's revelation is limited to the Bible. What was it that the apostles handed on to the churches they founded? The heritage of the apostles includes not only those things that eventually were written down in the sacred Scripture, but ". . . everything which contributes to the holiness of life, and the increase in faith of the People of God." From the example of the apostles, the Second Vatican Council concludes, "The Church, in her teaching, life, and worship, perpetuates and hands on to all generations all that she herself is, all that she believes" (**DV**, no. 8).

Catholics believe that God not only desires to hand on to us an inspired *written* Word, but a whole way of life and worship that includes all that the church is and believes. This includes, for example, how Christians are to worship God communally and beliefs about morality, especially moral issues not directly spoken of in Scripture.

These truths "handed on" within the church are known as "sacred Tradition," which God intends for all Christians for all times. The word "tradition" simply means something that has been passed on or handed on. The capital "T" in sacred Tradition designates those traditions in the church that are an essential part of God's revelation. They are not liable to change over time. Many other "traditions" in the church may change and often reflect a particular culture, time, or circumstance.

For example, sacred Tradition includes such things as the basic form of the Eucharistic liturgy that dates back to the primitive church, the teaching authority of ecumenical or worldwide councils of the churches' leaders. In the moral sphere, it includes the condemnation of abortion, infanticide, and the practice of homosexuality. These matters and others like them have been consistently addressed and practiced by Christians in a certain way for centuries, so Catholics consider them part of God's inspired and unchangeable Word to his church. God has not only given his church a written Word, but a way of life that needs to be presented, taught, and handed on. This is sacred Tradition.

Traditions (with a small "t") that are liable to change include such things as particular regulations for fasting and abstinence, the language and other outward forms of the liturgy—the wearing of veils or other conventions of dress that are often determined by the culture. These traditions are good and often necessary for a particular place and time, but not for all times and places. Celibacy is a requirement for priesthood in the Latin rite Catholic church, but not for all priests in Catholic churches of the Eastern rite. Thus it is an honored Catholic practice and tradition, though not part of sacred Tradition.

What is the relationship between Scripture and Tradition?

The Dogmatic Constitution on Divine Revelation explains that the Word of God is made up of both sacred Scripture and sacred Tradition, and that there is a close connection and communication between the two:

> For both of them, flowing from the same divine well-spring, in a certain way merge into a unity and tend toward the same end. For sacred Scripture is the Word of God inasmuch as it is consigned to writing under the inspiration of the divine spirit. To the successors of the apostles, sacred Tradition hands on in its full purity God's word, which was entrusted to the apostles by Christ the Lord and the Holy Spirit.... Consequently, it is not from sacred Scripture alone that the Church draws her certainty about everything which has been revealed. Therefore both sacred Tradition and sacred Scripture are to be accepted and venerated with the same sense of devotion and reverence (no. 9).

Is sacred Tradition unchanging?

Sacred Tradition is not static and unchanging, like the canon of Scripture. Sacred Tradition develops through the guidance of the Holy Spirit who is constantly leading the church into a fuller and a deeper understanding of the truth.

The church deepens and grows in its understanding of the truths handed down as its members study and pray over these things and seek to live them faithfully. There is also a deepening understanding of these truths, through the preaching and teaching of the church's leaders, particularly the bishops "who have received ... the sure gift of truth" (**DV**, no. 8). Indeed, the Council assures us that the church *is* constantly moving forward to a fuller grasp of divine truth until the Lord brings history to a close.

One example of deeper insights into God's truth discovered over the centuries concerns the *dignity of the human person*. The development of Christian teaching and social action regarding human rights is expressed in the church's stand against slavery and more recently abortion. In the area of *religious freedom,* the church teaches against coercion in religious matters, including bigoted religious intolerance and wars of religion. This is why many Christians strongly oppose apartheid in South Africa as an offense against human equality and dignity, and why Catholics are seeking an end to religious wars such as the prolonged conflicts in Northern Ireland (among Christians), and in the Middle East (among Jews, Arabs, Christians, and others).

Who decides the authentic meaning of Scripture and Tradition?

While biblical scholars, historians, and other experts can provide important insights into the meaning of God's Word, Catholics believe that God has given the charism (gift) and office of interpreting the authentic meaning of God's revelation to the successors of the apostles—the bishops in union with the successor of Peter, the pope—who are the official teachers or *magisterium* of the Catholic church.

In the history of our church, the universal body of bishops have always made the crucial decisions about God's Word. They first decided which ancient writings were truly God's revelation for all time (i.e., determined the "canon" of Scripture). They decided what Scripture actually meant, especially when disputes arose, as they met in Councils seeking the guidance of the Holy Spirit. And they have acted as the official teachers of the Christian faith in each age, as successors of Jesus' apostles.

The Dogmatic Constitution on Divine Revelation beautifully explains the role of the magisterium, and the close inter-relationship between sacred Scripture, sacred Tradition, and the magisterium. One point made very clear is that the teaching office or magisterium of the Catholic church ". . . is not above the word of God, but serves it, teaching only what has been handed on, listening to it devoutly, guarding it scrupulously, and explaining it faithfully by divine com-mission and with the help of the Holy Spirit; it draws from this one deposit of faith everything which it presents for belief as divinely revealed" (no. 10).

Like a tripod which cannot stand without each of its legs, the Word of God cannot stand and come to Christians in its purity and completeness without these three channels of God's truth: the Bible, sacred Tradition, and the teaching authority of the living church.

Is the Bible free from all error?

Why has God revealed himself to us? So that he may bring us into a relationship of love with himself through which we are saved from our sin and brought to eternal salvation—life with God forever in heaven. Hence, Catholics believe in biblical inerrancy—that the Bible is without error—*in all things that pertain to our salvation.* The constitution states: ". . . that the books of Scripture must be acknowledged as teaching firmly, faithfully, and without error that truth which God wanted put into the sacred writings for the sake of our salvation" (no. 11, also see no. 6).

In other words, although the Bible contains many true statements about astronomy, science, or political history, Scripture was not written for the purpose of teaching these things. Hence, any errors in fact about science or history, any literary mistakes, or any other contradictions in accounts or in matters of fact, do not prove that the Bible contains error in revealing all those things which are related to and necessary for our salvation. When the Bible speaks of God, the nature of human persons, God's will for them, the relationship of God to humanity, and how we are to relate to him and to each other, then there can be no error.

What is the relationship between the Old and New Testaments?

This relationship is well expressed in article 16 of *The Dogmatic Constitution on Divine Revelation.* In short, God's design is that "the New Testament be hidden in the Old and the Old be made manifest in the New."

What should be our attitude toward biblical scholarship?

This constitution instructs Catholics to interpret sacred Scripture with reference to three major sources. First, sound scholarship attempts to ascertain the author's intention in writing. The scholar does this by studying literary forms used (prophecy, poetry, didactic story, history, etc.), the prevailing *styles* of writing and narrating, and the *customs* of the time. All of these shed light on what God intends to say to us through the sacred writer.

Second, the scholar studies how each writing fits into the unity of the whole of Scripture and how it has been interpreted in the living tradition of the church, since ". . . holy Scripture must be read and interpreted according to the same Spirit by whom it was written, . . ." (**DV**, no. 12).

Third, the teaching office (*magisterium*) of the church is the final judge of the meaning of Scripture by virtue of its "divine commission and ministry of guarding and interpreting the word of God" (**DV**, no. 12).

Does this mean that Catholics must be scholars in order to read the Bible correctly and profitably? No. Catholics must respect and be open to learning from the insights of scholars. But Cardinal Ratzinger has pointed out that Vatican II's recommendation of sound biblical scholarship was not intended to make the Bible a "closed book," accessible only to experts. He points out that the foundational elements of our faith are not based upon the recent discoveries of biblical studies, "but on the Bible *just as it is* (his emphasis), as it has been read in the Church since the time of the Fathers until now. It is precisely the fidelity to this reading of the Bible that has given us the saints, who were often uneducated and, at any rate, frequently knew nothing about exegetical contexts. Yet they were the ones who understood it best."[1]

Reading the Bible in a spirit of faith and prayer as one well-instructed in the doctrine of the Catholic church normally would be an adequate safeguard against false interpretations. Study of the church's tradition of interpreting Scripture and using good scholarly resources enhances and deepens a person's understanding of God's Word. Various daily reading guides for Catholics, such as *The Word Among Us* and *God's Word Today,* are helpful resources for the layperson. Short Catholic commentaries, such as the series published by Liturgical Press in Collegeville, Minnesota, may also be helpful, although the quality and accuracy of individual commentaries differ in such series. Background articles in larger scholarly commentaries, such as *The Jerome Biblical Commentary,* may also be useful to the academically inclined reader.

Should we fear reading the Bible "too literally"?

The constitution does not answer this question directly. However, it affirms the "historical character" of the four

Gospels. The Council explains that while the authors of the Gospels did compile and edit their sources and shaped their writings to meet the situation of their churches, they did this "...always in such fashion that they told us the honest truth about Jesus" (no. 19).

We can conclude that the Gospels have an historical basis (i.e., they are neither "myths" nor fabricated stories). They tell us the truth about Jesus, regardless of how they were compiled, edited, or "shaped" by the evangelists.

Should we beware of "fundamentalists" or "liberal" interpreters of the Bible?

Certainly we should avoid labeling people as "fundamentalist" or "liberal" unless they themselves embrace these terms. *The Dogmatic Constitution on Divine Revelation* presents a carefully balanced approach to interpreting the Bible. It asserts the inerrancy of Scripture and the historical character and truth of the Gospels, while also urging the use of some modern methods of biblical scholarship to help us understand more fully what God and the sacred author intended to communicate.

The Council values the finding of scholars, yet reminds us that it is the God-given task of the church's teaching office to finally determine the authentic meaning of sacred Scripture if disputes or questions arise. By defining what interpretations of the Bible are unacceptable, the magisterium fixes limits within which scholars or readers are free to discover various interpretations and meanings of God's Word which are valid and profitable for Christian life.

Catholics must reject any interpretation of the Bible which denies either its human or divine character. As "the Word of God in the words of man," Catholics must recognize and obey the divine truth the Bible teaches. Yet we should also respect and employ sound scholarship which studies how God used the various modes of thinking and writing of the human authors to communicate the truth he wished to reveal for the sake of our salvation.

What place should reading and studying the Bible have in our lives?

Vatican II teaches that through the Bible, the heavenly Father "meets His children with great love and speaks with them" (**DV**, no. 21). It speaks of the Word of God as a source of strength, spiritual life, and food. Catholics should have "easy access to sacred Scripture" in "suitable and correct translations" (no. 22). Some translations that are accurate and popular among Catholics are the *Revised Standard Version* (RSV, Catholic Edition), the *New American Bible* (NAB with a recently revised New Testament), and the *Jerusalem Bible* (JB). [The reader should be aware that new translations have just been issued of both the *Revised Standard Version* and the *Jerusalem Bible.* These are titled respectively *The New Revised Standard Version with Apocrphya* (NRSV) and the *New Jerusalem Bible* (NJB).] Paraphrases such as the *Living Bible* are not generally accurate and are frequently misleading.

All the faithful, especially clergy and religious, are urged ". . . to learn by frequent reading of the divine Scriptures the 'excelling knowledge of Jesus Christ' (Phil 3:8)." Also, "prayer should accompany the reading of sacred Scripture, so that God and man may talk together" (no. 25).

Since the close of Vatican II, many Catholics have participated in a resurgence of reading and studying of Scripture which the Council has recommended, encouraged, and aided by a variety of new aids to Bible study and meditation. This is certainly a continual challenge which the Second Vatican Council lays before Catholics today. If the Bible is truly "the book of the Church," Catholics should love it, study it, and know it well.

As *The Dogmatic Constitution on Divine Revelation* exhorts us in its closing section: "In this way, therefore, through the reading and study of the sacred books, let 'the word of the Lord run and be glorified' (2 Thes 3:1) and let the treasure of revelation entrusted to the Church increasingly fill the hearts of men. Just as the life of the Church grows through persistent participation in the Eucharistic mystery, so we may hope for a new surge of spiritual vitality from intensified veneration for God's word, which 'lasts forever' (Is 40:8; cf. 1 Pt 1:23-25)" (no. 26).

RECOMMENDED READING

*The Dogmatic Constitution on Divine Revelation (**Dei Verbum**).* Abbott ed., pp. 111-128; Flannery ed., pp. 750-765.

QUESTIONS FOR GROUP DISCUSSION

1. Why has God chosen to reveal himself? What is our response to his revelation?

2. Why is Jesus the ultimate revelation of God?

3. How has God's revelation to the Hebrew people and to Jesus' apostles been transmitted to us today? How do we know that it has been passed on accurately?

4. What are the roles of sacred Scripture, sacred Tradition, and the teaching office (*magisterium*) of the Catholic church in passing on God's Word? How are they connected?

5. What do we mean when we say that the Bible is inspired by God and without error in all that concerns salvation?

6. What is the value of the Old Testament for Christians? Do the Gospels have a firm historical basis?

7. In studying and interpreting Scripture, what approaches and resources does this constitution recommend?

PERSONAL CHALLENGE

The major challenge presented to Catholics through *The Dogmatic Constitution on Divine Revelation* is to read and study God's Word, especially the written Word that is accessible to each of us in sacred Scripture.

Ask yourself, Do I read the Bible regularly? Do I really seek to understand it and apply it to my daily life? Do I need to develop a plan for Bible reading and study? Am I familiar with the sacred Tradition of the church? How could I become more familiar with what the church teaches about God's revelation? Do I respect the teaching office of the church—the pope and the bishops in union with him—as a faithful interpreter and guide to help me know God's revelation and apply it to my life?

RESOURCE LIST

Study Bibles

Note to the Reader: While all of the following study Bibles are helpful in different respects, there is no single "best" Catholic study Bible on the market. Therefore, before purchasing any study Bible, the reader should carefully examine what it has to offer, judging if it will meet his or her needs in study.

The Catholic Study Bible: uses the *New American Bible* text with the revised New Testament (Oxford).

New Jerusalem Bible: a totally new translation, following the principles of the earlier *Jerusalem Bible;* though not advertised as such, both the *JB* and *NJB* are good study Bibles (Doubleday).

The New Catholic Study Bible (not to be confused with *The Catholic Study Bible*): uses the *Today's English Version* translation (Our Sunday Visitor).

New Oxford Annotated Bible with Apocrypha: the standard study Bible using the *Revised Standard Version* of Scripture; it has been in use for almost twenty years (Oxford).

Helps for Bible Study

Reading Scripture as the Word of God, George Martin (Ann Arbor, MI: Servant, 1982).

God's Word to Israel, Joseph Jensen, O.S.B. (Wilmington, Delaware: Michael Glazier, 1982).

Jesus: A Gospel Portrait, Donald H. Senior, C.P. (Dayton, OH: Pflaum, 1975).

Periodicals for Daily Bible Reading and Study

The Word Among Us, P.O. Box 6003, Gaithersburg, MD 20844-0963.

God's Word Today, P.O. Box 7705, Ann Arbor, MI 48107.

For Studying Tradition

Basics of the Faith: A Catholic Catechism, Alan Schreck (Ann Arbor, MI: Servant, 1987).

The Church Teaches: Documents of the Church in English Translation, trans. by Jesuit Fathers of St. Mary's College (Rockford, IL: TAN Books & Publishers, 1973).

Faith of the Early Fathers, 3 vol.s, William S. Jurgens, ed. (Collegeville, MN: Liturgical Press, 1970).

TWO

The Church: A Mystery and the People of God

"THE MYSTERY OF THE CHURCH" is the title of the opening chapter of Vatican II's *Dogmatic Constitution on the Church* (*Lumen gentium*). But why is the church called a "mystery"? I have encountered Catholics who are convinced that the church is really not mysterious at all. They hold that it can be understood fully in sociological, political, and anthropological categories just like any other human institution. Some have even said that the church could be improved by eliminating any remaining "mysterious" elements and its outmoded hierarchical structure with the aim of modeling it after a modern political democracy. (I have even heard Catholics say that Vatican II calls for this change!)

These views neglect the fact that the church is *not* a purely human reality or product; it is also a work of God. Thus Catholics must discover and respect the nature of the church as God has established it. We cannot recreate or re-structure the church according to our own wisdom or preferences. The church is a mystery because it is, like Jesus Christ and sacred Scripture, a union of the divine and the human. It can never be reduced to a merely human organization.

Further, the church is a mystery because its membership includes not only those followers of Jesus Christ on earth, but also all those who have died in union with Christ: Mary and the saints in heaven, and the souls in purgatory.

There is more to the church than meets the eye, more than is visible. The church is a "communion of saints" that spans heaven and earth. The reported appearances of Mary or the saints throughout Christian history are reminders of the transcendent or "vertical" dimension of the church. As Catholics today rediscover the place of the angels, saints, and the Virgin Mary, as they encounter the Lord himself in prayer and in the liturgy, they are rediscovering the reality of the mystery of the church.

This challenging concept is followed up by Vatican II's presentation of the church as the "People of God" in chapter 2 of *The Dogmatic Constitution on the Church*. The church is a divine mystery, but on earth it appears as a group of ordinary people who are brought together and united in Jesus Christ, just as the first followers of Jesus were. The image of the church as the people of God tells us that "the church" is not just a building, nor is it limited to priests, religious sisters and brothers, or the pope. *All* the faithful, including the laity, are equally members of God's people, the church. This realization that, "*we* are the church," including equally each baptized member, was a great contribution of the Second Vatican Council to our understanding. Though our roles and tasks may differ, we who have been baptized into Christ have been baptized into one body and made one people. As St. Paul reminds us, we are "individually members of one another" (Rom 12:5; 1 Cor 12:27; Eph 4:25).

The Second Vatican Council challenges us to discover who we are. The church is *the* central topic of the Council. The four constitutions of Vatican II, which embody the Council's foundational teaching, all have to do with the church: the sources of its beliefs, its nature, its worship, and its place and mission in the modern world. *The Dogmatic*

Constitution on the Church (***Lumen gentium*** in Latin, meaning "Light of the Nations") presents in modern terms the Catholic church's understanding of herself, her own nature.

This constitution is like a hub of a wheel because it sets forth the fundamental doctrine of the church in a number of areas that are expanded and treated in more detail by other Council documents. In fact, no less than nine or ten of the sixteen Council documents have their basic teaching set forth in *The Dogmatic Constitution on the Church.*

For the sake of study, this constitution may be divided into three sections. The first two chapters deal with the nature of the church. The middle chapters describe specific ministries and vocations within the church. The last two chapters focus on the invisible and eschatological aspects of the church, especially the church as the communion of saints, with Mary as the church's model and mother. Let's pose some questions that capture the essence of each section.

What is the essence of the nature of the church?

It is not coincidental that the first chapter of *The Dogmatic Constitution on the Church* is entitled "The Mystery of the Church." As we have seen, the church is a *work of God* that cannot be reduced to a merely human reality, a mystery that cannot be adequately explained in sociological, anthropological, or political terms.

There are many reasons why the church is a mystery, but primarily because it is founded upon the work of Jesus Christ and the mystery of his cross and resurrection. Jesus is God's love present in human history. The church is a sacrament which makes God's love present in all ages and draws people into communion with him.

Jesus proclaimed the kingdom of God. The church represents the breaking forth of that kingdom on earth—not yet in its completed form, but like a seed budding and slowly growing amidst the trials and adversity of this world (**LG,** no. 5).

It is the mystery of a holy church made up of sinners always in need of purification and renewal, yet always striving to announce to the world the cross and death of the Lord until he comes (**LG,** no. 8, see 1 Cor 11:26).

The reality of the church is so rich that it is impossible to *define* precisely all that the church is. You can't define a mystery! We would do better to study the many images of the church found in the Old and New Testaments that describe various aspects of the church's nature, as the different facets of a precious stone show forth its rich beauty. The church is a sheepfold, a field, the "building of God," his temple, the "Jerusalem which is above," the bride of Christ, the spouse of the spotless Lamb, and "our Mother" (no. 6), just to mention a few biblical images.

Modern secular people have difficulty with the concept of mystery. We are uncomfortable if we can't define or explain something fully in rational terms. But the reality of the church reminds us that God is greater than our human intellect. The love he has shown in sending his only Son to redeem us and to make us his own people, his church, exceeds anything we could expect or imagine.

How is the church a communion?

"Communion" comes from the Greek word *koinonia,* which can mean community, fellowship, or unity. Acts 2:42 lists this oneness as one of the earliest characteristics of the church. The first Christians experienced fellowship or unity in their relationship with each other and with God.

The goal of the life of the church, as well as its richest fruit, is to build this close unity or fellowship among believers. Communion is not an emotion, but the realization of our oneness with God and with each other in Jesus Christ, which transcends all our differences and puts them in the proper perspective.

The Extraordinary Synod of Bishops of 1985 taught that this idea of communion is the key to understanding the church. The church is a communion with God through Jesus Christ and in the Holy Spirit. We *enter* this communion of the church through baptism, which is the foundation of our unity in Christ. Partaking in the Eucharist visibly expresses our unity and mysteriously makes us one through the power of God. The fact that we are in communion with each other in Christ also explains our relationships within the church better than an organizational chart showing "who does what." Even though there are many diverse roles and ministries in the church and some members exercise authority in their leadership roles in the church, the basic reality is that the church is a communion of believers in Jesus Christ sharing his life with each other and finding their unity in him (ES, p. 52).

What image does Vatican II use to describe the church?

In different ages, church leaders have chosen particular biblical images that epitomize how Catholics should look at the church. For centuries after the Council of Trent, the church often was viewed as the "perfect society" with clear teaching, structure, and order. In 1943, Pope Pius XII's encyclical letter on the mystical body of Christ shifted the focus away from the external structure and order of the church onto a new sense of the church as a living body of people founded by Christ. Members of the "body of Christ" are bound together in unity and charity, contributing their various gifts for the upbuilding of this body, as St. Paul had taught.

The Dogmatic Constitution on the Church does discuss the structure of the church (chapter 3), and the church as the body of Christ (no. 7). However, the chief image that the constitution presents for understanding the church today is as the "people of God." First Peter 2:9-10 states "... you are a chosen race, a royal priesthood, a holy nation, God's own people, ... Once you were no people but now you are God's people; once you had not received mercy but now you have received mercy."

The "people of God" image stresses that we are called together by God through an act of his mercy, and have been given a new identity as his people. Furthermore, *The Dogmatic Constitution on the Church* challenges our individualistic concept of salvation, as expressed in the question, "Have you been saved?" This document declares, "It has pleased God, however, to make men holy and save them not merely as individuals without any mutual bonds, but by making them into a single people, a people which acknowledges Him in truth and serves Him in holiness" (no. 9).

We are called to follow God as a people. The Council also reminds us that we are a *"pilgrim people of God"* who are never fully at home or "comfortable" in this world, but are ever striving to bring about and to enter God's kingdom. Our life on earth is a pilgrimage to God's eternal city—heaven. "For here we have no lasting city, but we seek the city which is to come" (Heb 13:14; see **LG**, no. 9).

Is the church still viewed as a hierarchy?

A common occurrence since Vatican II is for Catholics to downplay or reject the hierarchical structure of the church, or the church as the mystical body of Christ, because they think that these images are now outmoded or incompatible with the church as the "people of God." However, *The Dogmatic Constitution on the Church* makes it clear that the people of God is a hierarchically-ordered people. All of these images of the church are biblical and complementary, not in conflict or mutually exclusive. We must remember that

Vatican II *builds* upon past Catholic traditions and teachings rather than invalidates them.

Jesus Christ, who possessed both a divine and human nature, is the model for his body on earth. By virtue of God's indwelling, the church is also composed of both divine gifts and graces and the human structures and forms necessary to organize and live in this world as a society. The organizational structure of the church is not a merely human "power structure," but serves the Spirit of Christ, just as Christ's humanity served his divine nature. As we shall see later, offices in the church are intended to serve God and his people, not to "lord it over" others, nor to exalt those in office.

Who belongs to the people of God?

The Dogmatic Constitution on the Church makes a number of points related to this question that are at the heart of the Council's teaching. First, *"All . . . are called to belong to the new People of God"* (no. 13, emphasis mine). Membership in the church is open to all. The church is truly universal (catholic)—embracing all of humanity, for ". . . God . . . desires all men to be saved and to come to the knowledge of the truth" (1 Tm 2:4). Note that God's *desire* to save does not mean that all *will* be saved, nor does the statement that the church is *open* to all people mean that all *will* join the church.

Second, the church of Christ "constituted and organized in the world as a society, subsists [*subsistit*] in the Catholic Church, which is governed by the successor of Peter and by the bishops in union with that successor, although many elements of sanctification and of truth can be found outside of her visible structure. . . ." (**LG**, no 8). The word subsists is very important here.

One scholar says that more ink has been spilled over the word "subsists" than on any other word in the Council documents! In the past, it was common for Catholics to say that the Catholic church is the true church of Jesus Christ. At the Second Vatican Council, the bishops rejected this simple identification, which left no possibility of other Christian groups or bodies having *any* share in the church of Christ.

The word "subsists" means literally "to stand still, to stay, to continue, to remain." This particular word was chosen to indicate that the church Jesus founded has continued and will continue to exist in the Catholic church until the end of time, with all the essential marks of the church present (one, holy, catholic, and apostolic) and all the means of salvation available within her.[1]

Catholics, then, believe that only the Catholic church possesses the *fullness* of the church of Christ: all of the truth and all the means of salvation that Christ has entrusted to the church he founded (see also **LG**, no. 14). As we read, in this document: "They are *fully incorporated* into the society of the Church who, possessing the Spirit of Christ, accept her entire system and all the means of salvation given to her, and through union with her visible structure are joined to Christ, who rules her through the Supreme Pontiff and the bishops" (no. 14, emphasis mine).

The Catholic church is "linked" in many ways to other Christian churches and ecclesial bodies who possess many of the "elements of sanctification and truth" that belong to the church of Christ. These elements may include sacred Scripture, common beliefs, the sacraments, the office of bishop, Holy Eucharist, devotion to Mary, and numerous other devotions and beliefs.

Hence, it is possible to say that these Christians belong to the people of God, and yet in an incomplete or imperfect way from a Catholic standpoint, since they ". . . do not profess the faith in its entirety or do not preserve unity of communion with the successor of Peter" (**LG**, no. 15). When we discuss *The Decree on Ecumenism* in chapter 9, more will be said about other Christians and our relationship with them.

Finally, although they do not belong to the people of God,

Vatican II says that God's plan of salvation includes those who, through no fault of their own, do not yet know or embrace the gospel of Christ in whatever way it comes to them (**LG**, no. 16).

This refers to many who are not Christian. To the extent that these non-Christians embrace some aspects of the truth about God and respond to the grace of Christ, they are related to the new people of God, although they are not members of it because they do not believe in Jesus Christ nor have they been baptized into Christ and his church. In chapter 8 on the missionary challenge, we will discuss more fully the Council's teaching on non-Christians.

Are only Roman Catholics members of the Catholic church?

Those who formally call themselves "Roman Catholics" belong to the Roman or Latin rite of the Catholic church. Within the Catholic church there are a number of rites. These individual churches all submit to the pastoral guidance and authority of the pope, although they differ somewhat in liturgy, ecclesiastical discipline, and spiritual heritage. The Roman or Latin rite is by far the largest rite in terms of numbers and geographical extent, but the Second Vatican Council devoted a document to the Catholic churches of the various Eastern rites. *The Decree on Eastern Catholic Churches* declared that *all* rites of the Catholic church are "of equal dignity, so that none of them is superior to the others. . . ." (**OE**, no. 3).

The existence of these different rites adds to the richness and beauty of the Catholic church. The Extraordinary Synod of 1985 called attention to the great esteem that Catholics hold for the Eastern rite churches because of the richness of their traditions that date back to the apostles and come to us through the great Eastern theologians and "fathers" of the church (**ES**, p. 55). For instance, at the Second Vatican Council among the events that were most moving and instructive for the bishops were the celebrations of the Mass in different rites, according to their own customs. In one liturgy, the principal celebrant entered with a large hat shaped like a beehive. How surprised the Council Fathers were when the celebrant bent down and a deacon removed the offertory gifts from the headpiece! Instances such as this reminded the bishops just how diverse and rich were the rites and cultural expression of the Catholic church.

The existence of these Eastern Catholic churches is a sensitive issue for many Orthodox Christians, who view the existence of these "uniate" (in union with Rome) churches as an obstacle to Christian unity. They fear that through union with Rome, the Orthodox will lose their identity and heritage.

The Catholic church, however, believes that these Eastern rite Catholic churches have a special role to play in *promoting* Christian unity (see **OE**, no. 24, emphasis mine). They demonstrate that the Eastern churches, while having many practices differing greatly from the Latin rite, are encouraged to retain many of their own traditions and customs while belonging to the Catholic church.

To promote unity, the *Decree on Eastern Catholic Churches* (*Orientalium Ecclesiarum*) lists a number of ways that will make it easier for Eastern Catholics and Orthodox Christians to relate to each other. For example, it facilitates marriages between Catholics and Orthodox. But the regulations which prohibit full intercommunion between Catholics and Orthodox Christians must still be respected, until the day when the Lord brings us into full unity.

Since Catholics have the fullness of truth, do we have a ticket to heaven?

No. The Catholic church possesses this fullness, but not every Catholic takes full advantage of all that God offers to us in the church. Article 14 of this constitution explains that a

Catholic can be a member of the church in an external manner, but not "in his heart." We are warned that even a person with external membership in the church will not be saved if he or she does not persevere in charity.

The Council also warns against all inflated Catholic pride or "triumphalism," reminding us that whatever good resides within the church is solely due to the special grace of Christ. Moreover, Catholics will be judged more severely on the last day if they fail to respond fully in thought, word, and deed to the superabundance of grace and the means of grace that God has generously showered upon the Catholic church.

I tremble when I consider the extent to which Catholics in the West are neglecting many of the traditional means of receiving God's grace and growing in holiness: the sacraments, especially the sacrament of reconciliation and the Eucharist; prayer and fasting; almsgiving and other charitable works and works of mercy; and supporting one's parish through money, service, and active participation! God's judgment *will* begin with the household of God (1 Pt 4:17). Jesus himself instructed us: "Everyone to whom much is given, of him much will be required, . . ." (Lk 12:48).

Can only Catholics be saved?

The Dogmatic Constitution on the Church does state at one point that because Christ founded the Catholic church in order to save humanity, "Whosoever, therefore, knowing that the Catholic Church was made necessary by God through Jesus Christ, would refuse to enter her or to remain in her could not be saved"(no. 14).

The key word here is "knowing." God judges us according to whether we act on what we *know* as revealed by our conscience. If a person knows or recognizes that God made the Catholic church necessary for salvation, one would be condemned by God if he or she did not act according to that knowledge by remaining in or joining the Catholic church. Reasons of pride, fear, inconvenience, loss of friends, or social prestige might prevent a person from acting according to what they know is right. The Council is simply warning people that in a matter of salvation, one must act decisively regardless of the obstacles.

This teaching is very unpopular today because in Western culture we commonly view membership in a church as a matter of personal preference or convenience. But God's perspective is that belonging to his people is a matter of life and death—a matter of salvation.

Also we must understand that in rejecting the church, one is really rejecting Jesus, since Christ identifies himself with his body, the church. As the Lord told his disciples, "He who hears you hears me, and he who rejects you rejects me, and he who rejects me rejects him who sent me" (Lk 10:16).

We need to distinguish this belief from the error that only Catholics will be saved, since Vatican II's teaching clearly deals only with those who *know* or recognize that Christ founded the Catholic church and made her necessary for salvation. In the 1950s, a Catholic priest from Boston was even excommunicated for teaching that only Catholics can be saved.

How does God make his people holy?

The Dogmatic Constitution on the Church draws special attention to the sacraments (no. 11), to the proclamation of the Word of God (no. 12), and to the "charismatic" gifts of the Holy Spirit (listed in 1 Corinthians 12) as particular ways that the Holy Spirit, the sanctifier, makes God's people holy.

The constitution devotes an entire chapter to "The Call of the Whole Church to Holiness" to emphasize that holiness is for *everyone*. This holiness is expressed in somewhat different ways according to one's call as a single person, a married person, priest, deacon, or vowed religious.

The practice of the "evangelical counsels" of poverty, chastity, and obedience is praised by the document as a particular way in which holiness shines forth. In the midst of a world marked by materialism, obsession with sex, and rebellion against authority (even in the milder form of, "do your own thing"), these practices are a more powerful witness to Christ than ever.

Holiness is "a gift from Christ" and a fruit of the grace of the Holy Spirit in a person's life. Our task is to give our lives fully to God and to the service of our neighbor. This document teaches us that, "... *all* the faithful of Christ ... are called to the fullness of the Christian life and to the perfection of charity. By this holiness a more human way of life is promoted even in this earthly society" (no. 40).

The Extraordinary Synod of 1985 urges all Catholics to pursue holiness, which is an invitation to conversion and full participation in the life of God. Today so many people experience an emptiness that only God can fill. The church offers the only solution: discovering God through prayer, penance, adoration, sacrifice, self-giving, charity, and justice. It is the saints who have always led the way in the renewal of the church in the most difficult periods of its history. Today is no different. "Today, we have a tremendous need of saints, for whom we must assiduously implore God" (**ES**, p. 47). But through the Second Vatican Council we understand more clearly that holiness is for everyone. We are all called to be saints! The greatest challenge to Catholics, in this age and in every age, is to respond to this call.

How do we reflect the life of Jesus and share his mission?

The church carries on the three-fold ministry of Jesus as priest, prophet, and king. The first section of this constitution discusses how the church as a whole, as a "priestly people," continues this ministry of Jesus, while noting a distinction between the "common priesthood of the faithful" and "the ministerial or hierarchical priesthood." All of God's people are called to offer themselves to God as a "living sacrifice" (Rom 12:1) in union with Jesus Christ, but Jesus and the church set apart certain people to *lead* the people of God in their prayer and offering of themselves: those ordained to the ministerial priesthood. This ordained priesthood and the priesthood of the faithful are different but complementary ways of participating in the sacrificial priesthood of Christ, the great High Priest.

The second major section of *The Dogmatic Constitution on the Church* elaborates how this three-fold ministry of Christ is uniquely exercised by the church's ordained leaders, by the laity, and by those in the religious state.

Why does the church place so much emphasis on the ordained leaders?

Actually, it is noteworthy that *The Dogmatic Constitution on the Church* doesn't discuss the hierarchy of the church until the third chapter, *after* speaking of the mystery of the church and the people of God.

The Catholic church values the role of the ordained leaders because Jesus himself spent much time training and equipping his own apostles and then commissioned them in a special way to continue his ministry and to represent him as servants of their brethren—just as Christ came not to be served but to serve, and to lay down his life for his sheep. The document states that it is Jesus' will that the apostles' successors, "namely the bishops, should be shepherds in His Church even to the consummation of the world," with the successor of Peter as "a permanent and visible source and foundation of unity of faith and fellowship" (no. 18). (The role of these ordained leaders is spelled out in detail in three Vatican II documents that will be discussed later.)

Why isn't there a separate document on the pope?

The papacy is not given a separate document because the role of the papacy in the modern world was a primary focus of the First Vatican Council in 1869-70, which promulgated the decree on the pope's primacy (central position) and infallibility. Vatican II basically repeats what Vatican I taught concerning the pope's infallibility (teaching authority) and jurisdiction (governing authority), except that it speaks at greater length about the pope's unity with the "college" or body of bishops, of which he is both the head and a member. The pope and the bishops are joined into one body as Peter and the apostles were (**LG**, no. 22). However, as Vicar (representative) of Christ, and pastor of the whole church, the pope has "full, supreme, and universal power over the Church. And he can always exercise this power freely. . . ." (**LG**, no. 22).

I have heard critical comments about the pope intervening in the affairs of the church in a diocese, as if this were contrary to the Council. Clearly, this is not the case. Jesus Christ himself gave special authority to Peter (see Mt 16:18-19) and appointed him shepherd of the whole flock (see Jn 21:15 ff.). The pope must be ready to exercise that Petrine authority for the good of the church. The constitution says that the office of the pope shows forth the *unity* of the church, gathered around one head, while the bishops represent the variety and universality of God's people (no. 22).

How does Vatican II define "papal infallibility"?

Article 25 of *The Dogmatic Constitution on the Church* explains that infallibility is a gift of God to the church to insure that the deposit of divine revelation which God has entrusted to the church in matters of faith and morals will be faithfully preserved, interpreted, and handed on.

The Council presents three ways in which the church can propose a belief as infallibly true. First, repeating the teaching of the First Vatican Council (1869-70), the pope can define a doctrine infallibly regarding faith and morals when he proclaims this by a definitive act in his capacity as chief shepherd and teacher of all the faithful; that is, when he defines a doctrine *ex cathedra*, (from the chair of Peter).

Second, the universal body of bishops, teaching in union with the pope, can speak infallibly when "gathered together in an ecumenical council, they are teachers and judges of faith or morals," or even when scattered around the world "they concur in a single viewpoint as the one which must be held conclusively" (no. 25).

Third, the whole church can recognize a doctrine concerning faith or morals as infallibly true when through a supernatural sense of the faith (*sensus fidei*), "'from the bishops down to the last members of the laity,' [St. Augustine], it shows universal agreement . . ." (no. 12).

All of this flows from the promise of Jesus to send his Holy Spirit who would teach his followers all things and guide them into the fullness of truth (see John 14:25, 26; 16:12-15).

Those things which the church defines as infallibly true must be adhered to with the submission of faith. We *must* believe in them, because they are certainly true and direct our understanding of Christianity and our worship of God.

Some examples of doctrines formally defined by the church and considered infallible include the divinity of Jesus Christ, fully equal to the Father in Godhead (Council of Nicea, A.D. 325) the divinity of the Holy Spirit, co-equal to the Father and the Son in Godhead (Council of Constantinople, A.D. 381), that Jesus Christ is fully God and fully human (Council of Chalcedon, A.D. 451), that Mary is rightly called the "Mother of God" because she truly gave birth to Jesus Christ, the Son of God (Council of Ephesus, A.D. 431), that Mary was conceived without sin (the immaculate conception, Pope Pius IX, 1854) and was assumed body and soul into heaven (the assumption, Pope Pius XII, 1950).

But what about those things that do not fall into the category of infallible statements, which includes the vast majority of the teaching of the pope and our bishops? These include teachings on the application of the Gospel to the economy, social life, and politics; practical directives on fasting, support of Catholic education, and so on. *The Dogmatic Constitution on the Church* states that Catholics must accept the ordinary teaching of the bishops in matters of faith with "a religious assent of soul," and adhere to the pope's non-infallible teaching with the same attitude of "religious submission of will and of mind . . ." (no. 25).

In other words, by virtue of their office of teachers of the faithful, Catholics are to heed the ordinary teaching of the bishops and the pope with a disposition of assent to what they are teaching us. This is true even if we know that this teaching is not infallible.

Some Catholics wonder whether there are different levels of authority or importance among the many different teachings of the pope. There are. The constitution notes that the mind of the pope and the degree of solemnity or importance attached to his statements may be ascertained, "chiefly either from the character of the documents, from his frequent repetition of the same doctrine, or from his manner of speaking" (no. 25). Is the pope's teaching presented in the form of an encyclical letter, an apostolic exhortation, a letter, or an address to a particular audience?

In other words, all papal teaching, and to a lesser extent that of bishops and priests teaching in union with the pope, should be accepted by Catholics with an attitude of religious assent, but only matters formally defined by the church as infallibly true must be held with full submission as official doctrines of our faith. However, when the pope repeats a doctrine frequently, emphasizes a teaching as particularly important, or includes a doctrine in an encyclical letter or other more solemn mode of teaching, a Catholic knows that this teaching is very significant, even though not formally defined.

The teaching of the *magisterium* of the Catholic church, when not presented as infallible truth, is intended to form our consciences and help to conform them to the mind of Christ. That is why a disposition of assent, even toward non-infallible teachings, is so important for Catholics.

Later we will discuss how this understanding affects theological pluralism and the issue of dissent in the church.[2]

Wasn't "collegiality" a major theme of Vatican II?

Yes, collegiality was an important theme of the Council, and it is discussed most fully in chapter 3 of *The Dogmatic Constitution on the Church*. The theme of collegiality was important because Vatican I—forced to close early by a war—was unable to present a full picture of the Catholic hierarchy that included the bishops and priests. Vatican II's *Dogmatic Constitution on the Church* completes this picture by showing how bishops do work together as a team, along with their priests, in union with the pope.

The document explains that the apostles were formed by Jesus as a "college" or fixed group, with Peter singled out as head of this college under Christ himself (no. 19). To ensure that the mission of the apostles would continue until the end of the world, the apostles appointed successors who also formed a "college"—the college of bishops, with the successor of Peter, the pope, as their head under Christ.

As evidence for this collegiality, the document mentions, first, "the very ancient practice by which bishops . . . were linked with one another and with the Bishop of Rome by bonds of unity, charity, and peace" (no. 22). Second, councils of bishops, especially ecumenical (world-wide) councils "made common judgments about more profound matters." The full authority of the college of bishops over the church "is exercised in a solemn way through an ecumenical council" (no. 22). Third, they mention "the practice, intro-duced in ancient times, of summoning several bishops to take part in the elevation of someone newly elected to the ministry of the high priesthood" (no. 22). All of these are time-proven expressions of collegiality that continue in the church today.

The college of bishops, working together, "expresses the variety and *universality* of the people of God," but the college *always* must act in union with the head of the college, the pope, who represents and preserves the *unity* of the flock of Christ.

Is there a section devoted to permanent deacons?

Vatican II opened the door for the restoration of the ancient office of permanent deacon. Over the course of centuries, the office of deacon in the Catholic church became almost exclusively a stage in becoming a priest. Vatican II called for the restoration of ordination to the diaconate as a unique, permanent ministry of service in the church, as it had been in the first centuries of Christianity.

The institution of the permanent diaconate is left to the discretion of the bishops of each territory. As explained in *The Dogmatic Constitution of the Church*, this diaconate is "to be conferred upon men of more mature age, even upon those living in the married state" (no. 29). Those single men who are ordained to the diaconate must remain single and celibate in exercising their ministry as deacons.

What about the role of the laity in the church?

Another revolutionary aspect of the Second Vatican Council is that it is the first to directly address the ministry of the lay faithful, those neither ordained nor embracing religious vows. In addition to a chapter of this constitution, an entire document is devoted to the laity, entitled *The Decree on the Apostolate of the Laity* (see chapter 6 of this book). Vatican II truly ushered in the "age of the laity" in the Catholic church.

What is the role of the laity? In short, they are to carry out the mission of the church in the world of temporal or secular affairs. The laity carry out the mission of Christ and his church in the home and in the marketplace.

The constitution states, ". . . the laity, by their very vocation, seek the kingdom of God by engaging in temporal affairs and ordering them according to the plan of God" (no. 31). The laity "work for the sanctification of the world from within" like leaven. They make Christ known to others, "especially by the testimony of a life resplendent in faith, hope, and charity." Their call is to order earthly affairs of every sort according to the mind of Christ.

The lay faithful are commissioned and sent forth for this apostolic ministry, not just by the church, but by the Lord himself through the call and grace he gives them, especially through baptism, confirmation, and the Eucharist (no. 33). The constitution notes that the laity are sometimes the *only* ones who can bring the gospel of Christ into certain places or circumstances. They must respond generously to this call.

Finally, the laity "are in their own way made sharers in the priestly, prophetic, and kingly functions of Christ" (no. 31). This will be described fully in the chapter on the challenge to the laity.

What about the calling of religious in the church?

Religious are not to be distinguished primarily by the way they dress or by their title "brother," "sister," or "Father," but by the fact that they embrace a singular way of life within the church. They vow themselves to live out the evangelical counsels of poverty, celibate chastity, and obedience in a religious community and/or according to a particular rule that describes and guides their way of life.

The document notes that the religious life "is not an intermediate one between the clerical and lay states," but it includes both clerics and lay people who have heard and responded to God's call to follow Christ by living according to those counsels of Christian holiness (no. 43). The faithful living of these evangelical counsels is a sign that witnesses to the priority of the values of God's kingdom. Thus religious inspire all Christians to live out their own calling more fully.

The Council called for a renewal of those in religious life by re-discovering and returning to the ideal and spirit of their founders. Religious life must also be adapted in some ways to better serve the needs of people of this time. The Vatican II document, *The Decree on the Appropriate Renewal of Religious Life,* develops these themes in detail.

How do we prepare for the second coming of Christ?

With the sending of the Holy Spirit, the restoration of all things in Christ has begun. Thus *The Dogmatic Constitution on the Church* teaches, "The final age of the world has already come upon us" (no. 48). We are living in the "end times," the "last days." This final age of the world is the time between Jesus Christ's first coming as a man and his glorious second coming to judge the living and the dead.

Although God's reign on earth has already begun, it has not yet come to completion. The pilgrim church now lives in this world promoting the growth and values of God's kingdom, while looking forward with expectation and hope for Christ to return and bring his work to final fulfillment (see Col 1:15-20; 3:4).

In this interim period, the church is not passively waiting for Christ's return, but is striving to do his will in order "to please the Lord in all things (cf. 2 Cor 5:9)," and is engaged in spiritual warfare against Satan. "We put on the armor of God that we may be able to stand against the wiles of the devil and resist on the evil day (cf. Eph 6:11-13)" (**LG**, no. 48). These things, done in watchfulness as the Lord commanded, will enable us to stand with confidence before the judgment seat of Christ (no. 48).

Somehow many Catholics have gotten the impression that Vatican II does not teach or the Catholic church does not believe in the end times—the second coming of Christ and the last judgment, or Satan and the need to war against him. This notion certainly is not supported by this document, which confirms all of those truths, as they have also been taught by two of our most recent popes, Paul VI and John Paul II.

Who is included in the church?

The Dogmatic Constitution on the Church presents another dimension of the nature of the church. Until Christ returns in glory, the church not only includes those who are faithfully following Christ on earth, but also the "invisible Church": those who "have finished with this life and are being purified" (no. 49)—the souls in purgatory—and those in glory, the saints in heaven.

The constitution stresses that these three states of the church are united "in the same love for God and neighbor, and all sing the same hymn of glory to our God" (no. 49). In fact, the constitution asserts that the union between those in the church on earth and those who have died in Christ is not weakened, but actually *"strengthened* through the exchanging of spiritual goods" (no. 49). In Christ, we are clearly united to each other.

This mystery of the union of all who are in Christ is known as the "communion of saints." Those in the "church militant" on earth are "fighting the good fight of faith." Those in the "church suffering" in purgatory are experiencing the final cleansing or purification of venial sin and the effects of sin before entering heaven. Those in the "church triumphant" are enjoying the fullness of God's presence in heaven.

How does the communion of saints interact?

To summarize, the *saints in heaven* primarily help the church as they powerfully *intercede* for the rest of the church. Their prayer draws its strength from their close union with Christ. Their lives also provide an *inspiration* and an *example* for those in the church on earth. We, the church on earth, honor and venerate the saints—especially Mary the Mother of God, the apostles, martyrs—and the holy angels, and ask for their prayers (**LG**, no. 50).

The *church on earth* can strengthen and assist those in purgatory by praying for them, for it is "'a holy and wholesome thought to pray for the dead that they may be loosed from sins' (2 Macc 12:46)."

The visible and invisible church is bound together most closely in communion when we on earth gather to praise and worship God, especially in the sacred liturgy and the sacraments. In the Mass, we call to mind the presence of the saints in heaven and our union with them in worship. We also remember and pray for the dead, uniting our prayer for them with the one, perfect sacrifice of Christ on Calvary (**LG**, no. 50).

Each liturgy is a foretaste of the liturgy of consummate glory, which will occur when Christ returns. Each liturgy reminds us that all in the vast communion of saints, whether in heaven, on earth, or in purgatory, are joined together in Christ and in worshiping God the Father through Christ and in the Holy Spirit.

Don't devotions to the saints detract from worship of God?

The constitution reminds Catholics that authentic devotion to the saints "consists not so much in the multiplying of external acts, but rather in the intensity of our active love" (no. 51). What really counts is not how many devotions to the saints we have or prayers we say, but how well we follow their example of love of God and neighbor.

The constitution explains that our devotion to the saints does not weaken or detract from our worship of God, but "more thoroughly enriches the supreme worship we give to God the Father, through Christ, in the Spirit" (no. 51). God is glorified in his saints. When we honor them, we honor God and God's work in them. When we ask for their prayers, we recognize God working in and through them, because he hears the prayers of those who love him and have been faithful to him, especially the saints. God alone is to be worshiped, but the Father in heaven rejoices when he sees his children honoring and praying for each other.

Why is Mary called the mother of the church?

A lively debate occurred at the Second Vatican Council over whether a separate document should be devoted to Mary because of her importance in God's plan of salvation. Finally, the Council Fathers decided to place the teaching on Mary in *The Dogmatic Constitution on the Church* to underscore the fact that Mary is a part or a *member* of the church. The chapter on Mary is placed last in the document because truly Mary is a living summary or model of all that the church is. Mary *is* a member of the church, but certainly the preeminent one.

God formed a new covenant people, the church, because of the failure of most of his people of the old covenant to recognize and receive him. Mary represents the "New Israel," the new people of God, because she was the first to receive the Messiah by consenting to bear him in her own body. Not only was Mary the first to receive the eternal Word of God—Jesus—she also opened herself to receive every word he spoke. She is a model of faithful discipleship.

Mary is the model of the church as the people who believe in Jesus and who welcome and treasure his words and actions, and live according to them. Pope John Paul II in his encyclical letter on Mary (*Mother of the Redeemer*, **Redemptoris Mater**) took for his theme Luke 1:45: "Blessed is she who believed that the Lord would fulfill all that he had told her."

The Dogmatic Constitution on the Church presents a fully biblical treatment of Mary and her role in God's plan of salvation. The constitution is not giving a complete doctrine on Mary, nor deciding any "questions that have not yet been fully illuminated by the work of theologians" (no. 54).

What is Mary's role with regard to the church?

The constitution describes Mary as a *member* of the church, a *model* for the church, *mother* of the church, and *mediatrix* for the church praying to Christ for the church on our behalf.

Mary is "hailed as a pre-eminent and altogether singular *member* of the Church, and as the Church's *model* and excellent exemplar in faith and charity. Taught by the Holy Spirit, the Catholic Church honors her with filial affection and piety as a most beloved *mother*" (no. 53, emphasis mine).

Who intercedes more effectively for her children than a mother? And so the constitution also speaks of Mary as an intercessor or mediatrix for the church, but emphasizes that her mediation does not obscure or diminish the unique mediation of Christ (1 Tm 2:5-6). Rather her prayers "rest on His mediation, depend entirely on it, and draw all their power from it" (no. 60).

In recommending the title of "Mediatrix" for Mary, the constitution compares the use of this title with the use of "priest." Just as Christ is the one great High Priest for Christians (see Heb 4:14-15), this one priesthood of Christ is shared by both the ministers of the church, and in a different way by the laity. We all share, in different ways, in Christ's royal priesthood.

In a similar way the work of Christ, the one Mediator, is shared by him: in fullness with his mother, who opens the door to all graces by her prayer; and with all Christians and the saints who can pray to God through Christ for one another and for those in need (**DV**, no. 60).

God has richly blessed the church with a unique *member*, Mary, who is a *model* of its virtues, a *mother* given her by Christ to care for her needs, and forever a *mediatrix* of the grace of Christ through her powerful, motherly prayers on behalf of her children.

Don't some Catholics exaggerate Mary's role?

In the section on "Devotion to the Blessed Virgin Mary" (nos. 66, 67), the constitution acknowledges this danger, but notes that the honor given to Mary and the saints is essentially different from adoration which Catholics offer only to God. The document then goes on to warn against the two extremes of exaggerating Mary's role in God's plan, and of neglecting her through narrow-mindedness. Catholics are exhorted to study sacred Scripture and the fathers, doctors, and liturgies of the church, guided by the church's teaching office, in order to understand Mary's role more fully.

The constitution mentions that the Catholic teachings about Mary "are always related to Christ, the Source of all truth, sanctity, and piety" (no. 67). The document's section on Mary attempts to explain and clarify misconceptions about Mary's immaculate conception, (nos. 53 and 55), her role as model disciple and mother (no. 58), her assumption into heaven and queenship (no. 59), her intercessory role as "mediatrix" (nos. 60, 61), her virginity (no. 63), and her presence in heaven as a sign of hope and solace for God's people (no. 68). All of these teachings are related to Christ and his plan of salvation.

The Second Vatican Council recommends that all past teaching of the church about Mary be faithfully observed, but that all error or exaggeration be avoided, "Let the faithful remember moreover that true devotion consists neither in fruitless and passing emotion, nor in a certain vain credulity. Rather, it proceeds from true faith, by which we are led to know the excellence of the Mother of God, and are moved to filial love toward our mother and to the imitation of her virtues" (no. 67).

We also remember that Mary "unites and mirrors within herself the central truths of the faith. Hence, when she is being preached and venerated, she summons the faithful to her Son and His sacrifice, and to love for the Father" (no. 65).

How can the church be called both a "virgin" and a "mother"?

In the same way that Mary was. By her singlehearted devotion to the Lord, "the Church herself is a virgin, who keeps whole and pure the fidelity she has pledged to her Spouse. . . . She preserves with virginal purity an integral faith, a firm hope, and a sincere charity" (no. 64). The church becomes a mother "by accepting God's word in faith. For by her preaching and by baptism she brings forth to a new and immortal life, children who are conceived by the Holy Spirit and born of God" (no. 64).

Conclusion

The challenge to Catholics today is to recognize that *each* person—whether single, married, lay, religious, or ordained—is a full member of the church, the people of God. Each is called to holiness.

Unfortunately, we still witness in the church those who are dissatisfied, or those who think that they cannot contribute fully to the life of the church unless they are ordained or involved in a particular ministry. Such attitudes not only harm the individual, but perpetuate a false "clericalism" or other distorted understanding of the church.

Mary, a woman of faith and prayer, remains the ultimate model for the church—a model that all can imitate in our quest for holiness.

The Dogmatic Constitution on the Church reflects St. Paul's vision of a church with many members possessing different gifts and ministries, *all* of which contribute to the building up of the body. Paul's warnings about dissension, disunity, and party spirit as being opposed to the Spirit of God and the true nature of the church are also very timely today.

We are presented with a vision of a church which is rich and diverse: a church on earth longing for its home in heaven; the people of God possessing both divine gifts and a human form and structure; a church called to holiness with many ways of expressing and attaining it; a church including members in this world and in the next, united in a bond of love and service that transcends even death.

When is the church most fully what God has made her? It is in prayer, especially when her members gather around the Eucharistic table to once again re-present Jesus' sacrifice, which has made us one people of the new covenant in his blood. We will study the liturgy of the church in the next chapter. As we prepare, let us recall the words of Pope John Paul II: "The Council saw in the liturgy an epiphany of the Church: It is the Church at prayer. In celebrating divine worship, the Church gives expression to what she is: one, holy, catholic and apostolic."[3]

RECOMMENDED READING

Dogmatic Constitution on the Church (**Lumen gentium**), Abbott ed., pp. 14-96; Flannery ed., pp. 350-423.

(Optional: *The Decree on Eastern Catholic Churches* (**Orientalium Ecclesiarum**), Abbott ed., pp. 373-386; Flannery ed., pp. 441-451.

QUESTIONS FOR GROUP DISCUSSION

1. What does it mean that the church is a "mystery"? Why is this particularly important for a proper understanding of the church today?

2. Has the Council's emphasis on the church as the "people of God" affected the way you view the church? Explain.

3. Does the teaching on the church as the "people of God" change the Catholic church's basic teaching on the role and function of ordained leaders (the "hierarchy")?

4. What does it mean that *all* Catholics are equally called to holiness?

5. How do Catholics view the "end times" or the "last days"?

6. What place does Mary have in the life of the church and of each Catholic? Discuss her place in the church as a *member, model, mediatrix* (intercessor), and *mother.*

PERSONAL CHALLENGE

This constitution challenges us to reflect on the identity and nature of the church. We realize the significant role that each person has to play in the life of the church, which is the people of God.

Ask yourself: Do I understand the church as a work of God—a mystery—and not simply as another purely human organization? How has God called *me*—as a lay person, priest, and/or religious—to share in and carry on Jesus Christ's ministry of offering sacrifice to the Father (priest), proclaiming the Good News of God's kingdom (prophet), and extending God's rule or kingship (king) in the world?

How do I respond to God's call to be holy? What does the call to holiness mean to me? Do I recognize and act upon my living union in Christ with the souls in purgatory and the saints in heaven, as well as with my fellow Catholics and other Christians whom I see every day?

What place does Mary have in my life? Do I know her maternal care for me and for the whole church, as she desires to lead us into closer union with God through her Son, Jesus?

RESOURCE LIST

Mother of the Redeemer (**Redemptoris Mater**), Pope John Paul II

Credo of the People of God, Pope Paul VI

The Splendour of the Church, Henri De Lubac (San Francisco, CA: Ignatius, 1986).

The Church in the New Testament, Rudolph Schnackenburg (New York: Seabury, 1988).

Basics of the Faith: A Catholic Catechism (chs. 5, 9, and 10), Alan Schreck, (Ann Arbor, MI: Servant, 1987).

On the Primacy and Infallibility of the Pope (**Pastor Aeternus**), First Vatican Council, 1870.

THREE

Touching Eternity:
The Call to Worship

IT IS SO EASY TO LIVE a purely "horizontal" existence, constantly involved with the affairs of the world. But worship is the "vertical" dimension that reveals the meaning of all our earthly activity and gives our lives depth and purpose. God calls us daily to cease from our activity and to return to the source of our life, lifting our minds and hearts to him, the living God.

In the last chapter, we spoke of the church as the "communion of saints." When Christians worship, we join our prayer with the myriads of angels and all the saints in heaven who ceaselessly sing:

"Holy, holy, is the Lord God Almighty,
     who was and is and is to come!" **Rv 4:8**

"Worthy art thou, our Lord and God,
     to receive glory and honor and power,
     for thou didst create all things,
     and by thy will they existed and
     were created." **Rv 4:11**

69

"Worthy is the Lamb who was slain,
   to receive power and wealth and wisdom
   and might and honor and glory and blessing!" Rv 5:12

"Praise our God, all you his servants,
   you who fear him, small and great. . . .
Hallelujah! For the Lord our God
   the Almighty reigns.
Let us rejoice and exult and give him the
   glory, for the marriage of the
   Lamb has come, and his Bride
   has made herself ready . . ." Rv 19:6, 7

Worship is the subject of the Second Vatican Council's *Constitution on Sacred Liturgy*. Since worship is the only adequate response to God's revelation of himself and is the highest activity of the church, it is appropriate now to consider the liturgy. The church is primarily a worshiping community—a people called by God to be his own, full of adoration, praise, and thanksgiving for who he is and what he has done.

This is not self-evident, though. If one were to ask a Catholic today what is the most important activity of the church, some responses might be: feeding the hungry, caring for the sick and the dying, proclaiming the gospel to the unchurched, seeking justice and peace by overturning unjust social structures, or simply loving your neighbor.

Each of these are important ways of living the gospel, but *The Constitution on the Sacred Liturgy* affirms that the liturgy is "the summit toward which the activity of the Church is directed; at the same time it is the fountain from which all her power flows. For the goal of apostolic works is that all who are made sons of God by faith and baptism should come together to praise God in the midst of His Church, to take part in her sacrifice, and to eat the Lord's supper" (no. 10). Let us now consider why the church considers worship in the liturgy so important, and how we are to suitably worship God as his people.

How is the liturgy the summit of all our works?

What is the liturgy? Literally, it means "work of the people." It is the work of the people to offer to God all that we are and all that we do, in union with Jesus Christ. The liturgy, therefore, is not disconnected from our apostolic works, such as service of the poor, evangelism, love of neighbor, or the works of justice. Rather these efforts reach their fulfillment and find their true meaning when they are offered as sacrifices to the Father in union with the one perfect sacrifice of Christ on Calvary. In other words, it is only in the context of worship that all the other things we do as Catholic Christians make any sense and find their true meaning. For example, the great charitable work of Mother Teresa and the Missionaries of Charity, as well as that of countless other lay and religious communities, find their fulfillment and their source of power in prayer and the Eucharist.

We *all* come to worship God in the liturgy, bringing to him as our offering our whole selves and everything we do for love of him and our neighbor, just as Jesus Christ offered to the Father his whole life and all his works at the Last Supper and on Calvary. St. Paul writes, "I appeal to you, therefore, brethren, by the mercies of God, to present your bodies as a living sacrifice, holy and acceptable to God, which is your spiritual worship" (Rom 12:1).

How is this "living sacrifice" actually offered to God? *The Dogmatic Constitution on the Church* speaks of the way the laity exercise their share in Christ's priesthood by offering their lives to God each day:

For all their works, prayers, and apostolic endeavors, their ordinary married and family life, their daily labor, their mental and physical relaxation, if carried out in the Spirit, and even the hardships of life, if patiently borne—all of these become spiritual sacrifices acceptable to God through Jesus Christ (cf. 1 Pt 2:5). During the celebration of the Eucharist, these sacrifices are most lovingly offered to the Father along with the Lord's body. Thus, as worshipers whose every deed is holy, the laity consecrate the world itself to God. (no. 34)

At the offertory at Mass, each Catholic can offer their troubles, joys, and every aspect of life to the Father in union with Jesus' perfect offering of himself that is being celebrated and re-presented there.

How is the liturgy "the fountain" from which the church's power flows?

The church's power to carry out its mission in the world, and the power to make its own members holy, comes from Jesus Christ. Jesus comes to us and is given to us most fully in the liturgy of the Eucharist, in which we receive Christ's own body and blood. Indeed, *The Constitution on the Sacred Liturgy* says that through the liturgy the faithful "are given access to the stream of divine grace which flows from the paschal mystery of the passion, death, and resurrection of Christ, the fountain from which all the sacraments and sacramentals draw their power" (no. 61).

Hence, even though the liturgy is a fountain, the grace of the liturgy and the sacraments ultimately flows from the font of the cross of Jesus Christ. The liturgy and sacraments have no power or life of their own; they are channels of the grace of Christ.

Pope John Paul II has written that from the liturgy and the sacraments ". . . the faithful draw abundantly the water of grace which flows from the side of the crucified Christ. To use an image dear to Pope John XXIII, it is like the village fountain to which every generation comes to draw water ever living and fresh."[1]

While Catholics come to the liturgy ready to repent of their sins and to offer to God the sacrifices of their lives, they receive much more than they give. The faithful are nourished and strengthened by the Word of God and by Christ's body and blood, and then sent forth with new strength to live and work for God's kingdom.

To be nourished in this way, Catholics must listen attentively to the Word of God proclaimed and preached, and receive the Lamb of God in the Eucharist with faith and a desire to be guided, healed, and strengthened by him.

Are there any other reasons why the liturgy is so important?

Yes. The church basically exists to worship God. Worship is the one activity of the church that will never end—it is eternal. The constitution says that the earthly liturgy we celebrate is a foretaste and a sharing in "that heavenly liturgy which is celebrated in the holy city of Jerusalem [above] toward which we journey as pilgrims, ..." (no. 8). All other activities of the church will pass away, but worship of God lasts forever (see Rv 22:3-5).

Isn't this an exaggerated view of the importance of the liturgy?

The Constitution on Sacred Liturgy states that sacred liturgy "does *not* exhaust the entire activity of the church" (no. 9, emphasis mine) and that before people come to the liturgy "they must be called to faith and conversion" (no. 9). Important tasks of the church are, therefore, to preach faith and repentance, to prepare people for the sacraments, to teach them to obey God's law, and to "win them to all the works of charity, piety, and the apostolate" (no. 9).

The liturgy does not exist in a vacuum. It is now a

commonly recognized problem that many Catholics have been "sacramentalized, but not evangelized." They receive the sacraments of the church without a full faith in and commitment to Jesus Christ. It is also possible to participate in the liturgy without living out its grace and teaching in everyday life.

The constitution warns that ". . . in order that the sacred liturgy may produce its full effect, it is necessary that the faithful come to it with proper dispositions, that their thoughts match their words, and that they cooperate with divine grace lest they receive it in vain" (no. 11).

An important theological point is made here. Grace is always given by God in the sacraments and the liturgy. But any person may block the work of grace in his or her own life through lack of faith, rejection of God through serious sin, or other obstacles. In fact, St. Paul warned that whoever "eats the bread or drinks the cup of the Lord in an unworthy manner will be guilty of profaning the body and blood of the Lord. . . . For any one who eats and drinks without discerning the body eats and drinks judgment upon himself" (1 Cor 11:27, 29).

The Constitution on Sacred Liturgy also teaches that one who prays with the Christian community in the liturgy "must also enter into his chamber to pray to the Father in secret (cf. Mt 6:6), indeed, . . . he should pray without ceasing" (cf. 1 Thes 5:17) (**SC**, no. 12). Personal prayer is a necessary foundation for engaging in the prayer of the church. Cardinal Ratzinger says, "Eucharist presupposes personal prayer, prayer in the family, and extra-liturgical prayer in community" (*Ratzinger Report*, p. 134).

What's the purpose of Vatican II's reform of the liturgy?

The constitution states that the aim of this restoration of the liturgy is "the full, conscious, and active participation" of all the faithful in liturgical celebrations. The word translated "active" here more accurately means "real" participation—participation from the "heart" which could include silence as well as "activity," as the word "active" implies.

The Extraordinary Synod of Bishops of 1985 noted, "The active participation, so happily increased after the Council does not consist only in external activity, but above all in interior and spiritual participation. . . . It is evident that the liturgy must favor the sense of the sacred and make it shine forth. It must be permeated by the spirit of reverence, adoration and the glory of God" (ES, p. 52). Realizing that we are in the presence of God as a people in the liturgy, joined in worship with all the saints, Catholics should participate fully with attitudes of gratitude, joy, and prayerful reverence.

How was the restoration of the sacred liturgy to come about?

The constitution recognized that it was futile to hope for any change unless the *pastors* first became "thoroughly penetrated with the spirit and power of the liturgy, and become masters of it" (no. 14). From there, education of future priests in seminaries and the instruction of the laity could come about. Pope John Paul II has stressed that the future of the renewal of the liturgy still depends on the "biblical and liturgical formation of the People of God, both pastors and faithful" (VQ, no. 15).

What were some of the major elements of this restoration?

These are familiar to most people today, since "the liturgical renewal is the most visible fruit of the whole conciliar effort," (ES, p. 52) beginning with "turning the altar around so that the priest faces the people." The Council distinguished between the unchangeable elements of the liturgy and those subject to change (no. 21). Among the

' many changes called for by the Council were:

1. Streamlining rites so that they would be marked by "a noble simplicity," avoiding needless repetition and within the people's power of comprehension;
2. Emphasizing reading from holy Scripture, and advocating sermons drawing their content mainly from Scripture and liturgical sources;
3. The introduction of the vernacular language by the competent ecclesiastical authorities (usually the bishops) where they deemed this helpful in encouraging the faithful to understand the rites;
4. Involvement of different members (servers, lectors, commentators, musicians, where appropriate), and the establishment of liturgical commissions in parishes and dioceses;
5. Revisions of liturgical books and rites for the Mass and various sacraments;
6. Introduction of prayers that would increase the participation of the faithful, such as the "Prayer of the Faithful";
7. Concelebration of Mass as directed by the local bishop;
8. Restoration of the catechumenate for adults as in the early church (the RCIA);
9. "Extreme Unction" renamed the "Anointing of the Sick" and administered to those in danger of death, not only at the point of death;
10. New emphasis on praying the "Liturgy of the Hours" (the Divine Office) by lay people and in parishes, as well as by clergy and religious;
11. Revision of the calendar of the liturgical year, with special emphasis on Sunday, the Lord's Day, as "the foundation and nucleus of the whole liturgical year" (no. 106);
12. Changes in laws regarding fast and abstinence, placing

more responsibility on the individual;

13. Adaptation of the liturgy, within some specified boundaries, to different cultures;

14. Revisions and some new directions for sacred music, sacred art, and sacred furnishings.

Do we understand the presence of Christ in the liturgy any differently?

Before the Second Vatican Council, many Catholics would only think of Christ's presence at Mass, for example, as being in the *Eucharist* at Holy Communion and in the tabernacle, and perhaps also in the *priest* who represents Christ. In addition to these modes of Christ's presence, this constitution reminds the faithful that Christ is also present in the *other sacraments,* such as baptism, in *God's Word* which is proclaimed, and in *his people* gathered to pray and sing.

Jesus himself promised, "For where two or three are gathered in my name, there am I in the midst of them (Mt 18:20)" (no. 7). Pope John Paul II has said that this presence of Christ in the Christian assembly gives it a unique character, with the consequent duties of brotherly welcome, forgiveness (cf. Mt 5:23, 24), and dignity in behavior, gesture, and song (**VQ**, no. 7).

What does the constitution say about the Mass as a sacrifice?

Certainly the death of Christ on the cross is the one sacrifice that redeems the human race. This constitution declares that at the Last Supper Jesus instituted the Eucharistic sacrifice of his body and blood "in order to *perpetuate* [that is, to continue or to 're-present'] the sacrifice of the Cross throughout the centuries until He should come again" (emphasis mine). The church is entrusted with "a memorial of His death and resurrection: a sacrament of love, a sign of unity, a bond of charity, a paschal banquet in which

Christ is consumed, the mind is filled with grace, and a pledge of future glory is given to us" (no. 47).

The Eucharist perpetuates and makes present to us in sacramental form the one eternal sacrifice of Christ on Calvary. In this sense, the Eucharist is a *memorial* of Jesus' death and resurrection. But it is also a *living* memorial in which the one being remembered is actually present to us under the appearance of bread and wine. Jesus is not re-sacrificed, but the event of Christ's one sacrifice, which transcends time, is made present to us, and his body and blood really given to us in sacramental form.

Pope John Paul II has recognized the re-enactment of the Paschal Mystery of Christ in the liturgy as the central topic of this constitution, especially Christ's presence in the Eucharist. The pope urges pastors to teach frequently about the real presence of Christ in the Eucharist in their cate-chetical instructions, calls the faithful to live it out, and encourages theologians to expound on it. He also notes: "Faith in this presence of the Lord involves an outward sign of respect toward the church, the holy place in which God manifests himself in mystery (cf. Ex 3:5), especially during the celebration of the sacraments: Holy things must always be treated in a holy manner" (VQ, no. 7).

Was the teaching on the Word of God in the liturgy a major change?

Yes. Although the reading of sacred Scripture had always been a part of the sacred liturgy, Vatican II underscores that the Liturgy of the Word and the Liturgy of the Eucharist are *both* the bread of life for God's people DV, no. 21). They "are so closely connected with each other that they form but one single act of worship" (SC, no. 56). *The Constitution on the Sacred Liturgy* insists that if the restoration of the sacred liturgy is to be achieved, a "warm and living love for Scripture" must be promoted (no. 24). "There is to be more reading from holy Scripture, and it is to be more varied and suitable" (no. 35 and see no. 51). Further, the sermon should draw its content mainly from scriptural and liturgical sources, and Bible services should be encouraged (no. 35).

In 1988, the Pope noted that the Word of God is now better known by Catholics, but there are new challenges: the need for faithfulness to the authentic meaning of the Scriptures, especially in good translations; proclaiming the Word of God as truly *God's* Word; prayer and study of Scripture for ministers of the Word and homilists; and an effort on the part of the faithful to seek out God's Word, to pray and study it, in order to discover Christ (**VQ**, no. 8).

The Pope also warns: "Since the liturgy is totally permeated by the word of God, any other word must be in harmony with it, above all in the homily but also in the various interventions of the minister and in the hymns which are sung. No other reading may supplant the biblical word, and the words of men must be at the service of the word of God without obscuring it" (**VQ**, no. 10).

How do popular devotions fit into this understanding?

While most popular devotions are "warmly commended," they are subordinate to the liturgy. As the prayer of the whole church, "the liturgy by its very nature far surpasses any of them" (**SC**, no. 13). Pope John Paul II is more cautious in his evaluation of popular devotion, speaking of a need for them to become ever more mature and authentic acts of faith. In general, popular devotions are welcomed and encouraged. ". . . the liturgy will build upon the riches of popular piety, purifying and directing them toward the liturgy as the offering of the peoples" (**VQ**, no. 18).

Has the restoration of the liturgy been successful?

Pope John Paul II wrote in his letter on the Eucharist: "A very close and organic bond exists between the renewal of the liturgy and the renewal of the whole life of the Church."[2]

Although the reform of the liturgy has encountered many difficulties and has not yet been fully accomplished, I would agree with Pope John Paul II who observed that the vast majority of the pastors and the Christian people have accepted the liturgical reform in a spirit of obedience and indeed joyful fervor. He notes that for many people the message of the Second Vatican Council has been experienced principally through the liturgical reform (**VQ**, no. 12).

What has been the greatest concern regarding liturgical renewal?

The greatest concern among church leaders such as Cardinal Ratzinger and many of the bishops at the Extraordinary Synod is this: has the church experienced a loss of the sense of the sacred in the liturgy, and a loss of the sense of the mystery of God present in the church?

The Extraordinary Synod in its *Final Report* speaks of a secularism or immanentism which denies the dimension of mystery, but notes that "signs of a return to the sacred also exist. Today, in fact, there are signs of a new hunger and thirst for the transcendent and divine. In order to favor this return to the sacred and to overcome secularism, we must open the way to the dimension of the 'divine' or of mystery and offer the preambles of faith to mankind today. . . . Does not the spread of sects perhaps lead us to ask whether we have sometimes failed to sufficiently manifest the sense of the sacred?" (**ES**, pp. 44-45).

The Synod states that the liturgy always must favor the sense of the sacred and make it shine forth, permeated by the spirit of reverence, adoration, and the glory of God" (**ES**, p. 52).

Why has the liturgy seemed to have lost its sense of "sacredness"?

There are various opinions about this. Some think that the shift of the language to the vernacular made the liturgy too familiar or common. The Council never mandated the abolition of the Latin language, but allowed the introduction of the vernacular at the discretion of the bishops. Most bishops and episcopal conferences, of course, elected to change to the vernacular in order to promote the full, conscious, and active participation of the faithful, which was the primary goal of the liturgical renewal. (Unfortunately, we know that some traditionalists, led by Marcel Le Febvre, mistakenly understood the Latin language as one of the unchangeable elements of the liturgy, which has led to their rejection of the liturgical reform and schism from the Catholic church.)

Cardinal Ratzinger argues that we must preserve the beauty of sacred music, rather than settling for "utility music." He also reminds us that the liturgy is not a show or a spectacle to be made by men and women, but consists in solemn repetitions. "It cannot be an expression of what is current and transitory, for it expresses the mystery of the Holy" (*Ratzinger Report*, p. 126).

It is true that some of the difficulties with the liturgy have been caused by experimentation and innovations in violation of article 22 of *The Constitution on the Sacred Liturgy* which prohibits anyone but the bishop or the pope to change anything in the liturgy on their own authority. Many Catholics have experienced abuses in which parts of the canon of the Mass have been offered or modified. Pope John Paul II explains that the difficulty with this is that liturgical celebrations "are not private acts, but 'celebrations of the Church,' the 'sacrament of unity,'" which belongs to the whole body of the church. This is why no priest or group is permitted to add, subtract, or change anything in the liturgy on their own initiative. He specifically mentions that no one is allowed to compose their own Eucharistic Prayers or substitute other readings for sacred Scripture. These actions are in direct contradiction to the genuine reform of the liturgy and "deprive the Christian people of the genuine treasures of the liturgy of the Church." Pope John Paul calls for bishops to root out such abuses (**VQ**, no.s 10 and 13).

What can be done to restore the "sacredness" of the liturgy?

The liturgy is a gift of God to the church, as well as the "work of the people." We observe many people flocking to Christian churches or fellowships which emphasize in some way the sacred and divine aspects of Christianity, such as the transcendence of God, the holiness of the Word of God, and the gifts of God. Sadly, we also see people seeking spiritual reality in cults like New Age religions which promise initiation into the sacred, but which actually counterfeit true religion—or may even be demonic.

Yet the Catholic church offers in her liturgy the real presence of the one true God, as well as the worship he desires, centered on the paschal mystery of Jesus Christ, the Son of God and our Savior. This is a major reason why so many people are attracted to the Catholic church—because God and Christ are truly present there and given authentic worship. As Cardinal Ratzinger comments about the liturgy, "... [it] does not come from what *we do* but from the fact that something is *taking place* here that all of us together cannot 'make.' In the liturgy there is a power, an energy at work which not even the Church as a whole can generate: what it manifests is the Wholly Other ..." (*Ratzinger Report*, p. 126).

For this reason, Catholics do not need to worry about the liturgy itself losing its sacredness. This sacredness can be obscured, or even effaced, if the liturgy is distorted in such a way that it is no longer the prayer of the church, as the pope has warned. But if what is celebrated is truly the prayer of the church, it *is* sacred because Christ is present there in all the ways we have described.

In order for those who participate in the liturgy to discern the presence of God and to benefit from the graces available there, they must come with the appropriate attitudes and dispositions of heart and mind. God will not force his way into anyone's heart. Therefore, the faithful must be instructed and called to approach the liturgy with faith, repentant hearts, and a desire to worship.

You might say, then, that we don't have to change the liturgy; the liturgy needs to change us! And it will, if our hearts are open. The mighty, loving, all-holy God is present there. This is why *The Constitution on the Sacred Liturgy* stresses that Catholics must be properly *instructed* in the meaning of the liturgy, so they can approach God with reverence.

For example, we will never appreciate the liturgy fully if our focus is on how much we are being uplifted, or worse, entertained. Our focus should be on worshiping God, placing ourselves in his presence through prayer, and seeking to gain as much as we can from the celebration and the homily.

On the other hand, the Council stresses the need for the celebrants, ministers, and those who plan and lead the liturgy to make God's presence as accessible and evident as they can. They need to prepare well and conduct themselves with authentic reverence and respect for the mysteries they are celebrating and proclaiming. These efforts are not to be equated with the "sacredness" of the liturgy, since that depends on God's presence. However, these efforts certainly can enhance the beauty and majesty of the liturgy. They will help the faithful enter into worship more easily.

What are some directions for the ongoing renewal of the liturgy?

The basic challenge for Catholics today is to continue to implement the authentic teaching of the constitution in ways and areas where it has not yet been fully carried out.

Practically, every Catholic could benefit personally from more instruction in the liturgy and greater efforts to participate in the liturgy and sacraments of the church. We all need to deepen our personal prayer and family prayer, which enriches the liturgical worship of the church community.

Pope John Paul II, in 1988, suggested some directions and areas for future renewal of the liturgy in the church. These include:

1. "A new and intensive education in order to discover all the richness contained in the liturgy" (**DC**, no. 9);
2. Ongoing biblical and liturgical formation programs for seminarians, for priests throughout their ministries, and for lay people (**VQ**, no. 15);
3. The adaptation of the liturgy to different cultures, welcoming expressions which are compatible with the authentic spirit of the liturgy, with respect for the substantial unity of the Roman rite. "Cultural adaptation also requires conversion of heart and even, where necessary, a breaking with ancestral customs incompatible with the Catholic Faith" (**VQ**, no. 16);
4. A response in liturgical renewal to new problems such as: "the exercise of a diaconate open to married men; liturgical tasks in celebrations which can be entrusted to lay people; liturgical celebrations for children, for young people, and the handicapped." and so on (**VQ**, no. 17).

As the Holy Father has said, the time has come to renew that spirit of worship that was so powerful at the time of the Council. "The seed was sown: It has known the rigors of winter, but the seed has sprouted and become a tree. It is a matter of the organic growth of a tree becoming ever stronger—the deeper it sinks into the soil of tradition" (**VQ**, no. 23). Truly this renewal will bear fruit, for worship is a gift of God to the church, a gift that will endure and continue forever in heaven.

Just as the Second Vatican Council challenged Catholics to a new level of participation in worship, so too it has challenged us to a new intensity of participation and involvement in the modern world. Through the liturgy, Catholics are strengthened in their worship of God to do the will of God. They are sent forth with the commission: "Go in peace, to love and serve the Lord." Through the nourishment which the liturgy and prayer provides, Catholics should desire to go forth in peace to transform the world for Christ. The next chapter on *The Pastoral Constitution on the Church in the Modern World,* presents the church with the direction and guidance it needs to undertake this challenging mission.

RECOMMENDED READING

The Constitution on Sacred Liturgy (*Sacrosanctum concilium*). Abbott ed., pp. 137-138; Flannery ed., pp. 1-37.

QUESTIONS FOR GROUP DISCUSSION

1. What does it mean that the liturgy "is the summit toward which the activity of the Church is directed" and "the fountain from which all her power flows" (no. 10)?

2. Is there "full, conscious and active participation" of the faithful in liturgical celebrations in your parish? Or is there still more that needs to be done? Discuss.

3. What things are necessary for the faithful to benefit fully from the liturgy?

4. How do Catholics understand the presence of Christ in the Holy Eucharist? How should we respond to those who claim that in the Mass we are again sacrificing Christ?

5. Is it true that we've lost a sense of sacredness in the liturgy? Discuss.

6. Besides the Mass itself, what other aspects of worship have changed significantly since Vatican II? This could include other sacraments, sacramentals, devotions, the liturgical year, use of the liturgy of the hours, church music, art, and architecture.

PERSONAL CHALLENGE

The Second Vatican Council teaches that worship is at the heart of the life of the church and the life of each Christian. Ask yourself: Do I see the value in worship, both personal prayer and the common worship or liturgy of the church? Is going to Mass and other liturgical services just a habit or a duty? Or do I realize that God is offering me something special there? How can I make more room in my life for prayer and worship?

When I do attend Mass or other services, do I prepare myself and participate in a way that honors God and helps me to get the fullest benefit out of the liturgy? Or do I often just go through the motions? What would help me to enter more fully into my prayer and the liturgy?

Do I understand the liturgy, the sacraments, and other aspects of the church's worship? Would some further study help me to appreciate it more? What do I expect to get out of the liturgy? After studying and discussing this document, have my expectations changed? Is there anything I can contribute to my parish or religious community to support or enhance its liturgical worship?

RESOURCE LIST

The Bible and the Liturgy, Jean Danielou (Ann Arbor, MI: Servant, 1979).

On the Mystery and Worship of the Eucharist, (Dominicae Cenae), Pope John Paul II, Feb. 24, 1980.

Christian Prayer Through the Centuries, Josef Jungmann (New York: Paulist, 1978).

The Mass, Josef Jungmann (Collegeville, MN: Liturgical Press, 1976).

The Bible and the Mass, Peter Stravinskas (Ann Arbor, MI: Servant, 1989).

The Eucharistic Essence, Form and Celebration, Johannes Emminghaus (Collegeville, MN: Liturgical Press, 1978).

Redeemed Creation: The Sacramentals Today, Laurence Brett (Michael Glazier Press, Message of the Sacraments Series, Vol. 8).

FOUR

How Should a Catholic Act in the World?

A S THE TWENTIETH CENTURY closes, monumental issues regarding the dignity and rights of individual persons and the future of the world itself press upon us. Will regional wars continue to cause worldwide instability and anxiety, or will a nuclear conflagration engulf us? Will the opening of the Communist world lead to a flourishing of spiritual and human values and conversion to Christ—or to the decadence, materialism, and secularization that has infected the West? Will the global assault against human life continue through the plagues of abortion, euthanasia, and other flagrant violations of human rights and dignity? Will world poverty and hunger increase?

Catholics know that they cannot escape these issues and are challenged to decide where and how to respond to them. For example, how does a Christian respond when the law of the land allows abortion on demand? Should one picket, send petitions and support politicians who oppose abortion, block abortion clinic entrances, pray, contribute to right-to-life organizations, or even march on Washington, D.C.?

Perhaps this paints too bleak a picture. There are positive signs that the consciences of people throughout the world are being awakened. The longings of the human heart for peace, justice, and the preservation of human life are being aroused as people begin to work together for those goals.

Pessimism or optimism? Which marks the Catholic's view of the modern world? In studying the Second Vatican Council's *Pastoral Constitution on the Church in the Modern World,* the answer emerges that Catholics are to be neither optimists nor pessimists about the world, but are to possess a *realism marked by Christian hope.* This document presents the condition of the world with a stark realism. Yet the last word—the word of hope—is that Jesus Christ is present and has redeemed the world.

Christ and his Holy Spirit offer us specific guidance, through the church, about how we should view the modern world and act within it so that God's kingdom will break forth there more fully. The challenge to Catholics is to seek and to hear God's guidance and wisdom, and then to *act* according to it in the world.

The Pastoral Constitution on the Church in the Modern World is a unique document in many ways. Initially, there were no plans for such a document by the preparatory commissions or by the pope. But "Schema 13" emerged from the floor of the Council at the urging of Bishop Dom Helder Camara of Brazil, with the support of Cardinal Leon-Josef Suenens of Belgium and Cardinal Montini (Pope Paul VI). They thought it would be incredible that a Council which hoped to place the church in touch with the modern world should fail to issue a document on how Catholics were to view and respond to the actual conditions of modern society. This certainly was in keeping with the purpose and vision of the Council set by Pope John XXIII, even though he had not explicitly called for such a document. Thus this constitution was born.

This is the only constitution explicitly addressed to the whole world and not only to Catholics. It is the only "pastoral" constitution issued. This longest document of the Council is divided into two parts: the first setting forth the *principles* of the Catholic understanding of the modern world and involvement in it; the second discussing *specific areas* where the church is challenged today to become involved, providing leadership and guidance. This chapter will deal with the first part: how Catholics understand the modern world and their involvement in it. What are the guiding principles and values that this constitution presents?

Are Catholics to identify with the modern world?

The document begins with the understanding that Catholics are to *identify* themselves with the modern world, because they are part of it and share its life. "The joys and hopes [hence the Latin title, *Gaudium et spes*], the griefs and anxieties of the men of this age, especially those who are poor or in any way afflicted, these too are the joys and hopes, the griefs and anxieties of the followers of Christ. Indeed, nothing genuinely human fails to raise an echo in their hearts" (no. 1).

What is the reason for getting involved?

Catholics have a specific understanding of the nature of humanity and the world which is the foundation for all their involvements. The constitution says that "the pivotal point of our total presentation will be *man himself*, whole and entire, body and soul, heart and conscience, mind and will" (no. 3, emphasis mine). This truth about humanity also includes what Catholics know through divine revelation. Christians see the world "as created and sustained by its Maker's love, fallen indeed into the bondage of sin, yet emancipated now by Christ. He was crucified and rose again to break the stranglehold of personified Evil [Satan], so that this world might be fashioned anew according to God's design and reach its fulfillment" (no. 2).

So the church offers its assistance to foster the true

meaning and brotherhood of all people. The people of God carry on the mission of Christ: to seek and to save those who are lost. "Inspired by no earthly ambition, the Church seeks but a solitary goal: to carry forward the work of Christ Himself under the lead of the befriending Spirit. And Christ entered this world to give witness to the truth, to rescue and not to sit in judgment, to serve and not to be served" (no. 3).

This is the heart of the "Catholic Challenge" in the modern world.

How do we evaluate the present condition of society?

In order to know specifically how to act in different circumstances, the church has the duty of "scrutinizing the signs of the times and of interpreting them in the light of the gospel" (**GS**, no. 4). Too often people just flow with the times and unthinkingly follow whatever trend of thought or behavior is currently fashionable or popular. Catholics need to discern and test these things according to the standard of the gospel of Jesus Christ.

In discerning the "signs of the times," the constitution noted a number of disturbing imbalances and paradoxes. Never have wealth, resources, and economic power been greater, yet a huge proportion of the world's population is starving and illiterate. Never has the world been so keenly aware of freedom, yet new forms of social, psychological, and economic slavery continually appear. Never has humanity been so aware of the unity of the human race, the "global village," yet wars and conflicts continue to abound. Ironically, "man painstakingly searches for a better world, without working with equal zeal for the betterment of his own spirit" (no. 4). These imbalances reflect what Blaise Pascal termed "the greatness and wretchedness of man."

After the constitution describes these challenges and choices that face human freedom today, it notes that these difficulties are linked with "that more basic imbalance rooted in the heart of man. For in man himself many elements wrestle with one another" (no. 10). As St. Paul described so well in Romans 7, the root of humanity's struggle lies within each human heart.

People are again asking themselves the most basic questions: What is humanity? Why do we suffer? What is the purpose of our efforts toward progress? What can people offer to human society and what can they hope to receive? What happens to us after death?

The introduction of this constitution ends with the word of hope: the church believes that Christ can, through his Spirit, "offer man the light and the strength to measure up to his supreme destiny" (no. 10).

What about the nature of the human person?

Many humanists and even atheists agree with Christians that "all things on earth should be related to man as their center and crown" (no. 12). But not all agree about the nature of humanity. The first of *The Pastoral Constitution on the Church in the Modern World* presents an excellent summary of basic Christian teaching about the human person. Topics include: our goodness and dignity; the reality of sin which has corrupted human nature and cast us into "a dramatic struggle between good and evil, between light and darkness" (no. 13); and the hope that humanity has in the redemption of Christ who "came to free and strengthen man, renewing him inwardly and casting out the prince of this world (cf. Jn 12:31) who held him in the bondage of sin" (no. 13).

The presentation hinges around the inherent goodness and dignity of the human person, who "by his interior qualities, outstrips the whole sum of mere things." Far from being just a meaningless speck in a vast universe, the human person is loved by God and possesses an immortal soul. A single human person is more precious and valuable in God's eyes than the sum of all merely material things in the universe put together. Christ died to save each individual person. This is the root of the Catholic understanding of the dignity of the human person and explains why Catholics are opposed to any activity that unjustly and needlessly threatens or destroys human life, such as abortion, euthanasia, wars of aggression, and the like. From the moment of conception, each person is called by God to the fullness of life in this world and to eternal life and joy in heaven.

The constitution teaches that each person is created by God as good and precious to him. The evil and rebelliousness that stirs within us due to sin does not negate the dignity of the person, but indicates that each person must strive to resist sin and evil and instead "glorify God in his body" (no. 14).

The constitution illustrates the dignity of the person by decribing his or her various attributes: the dignity of the *mind,* which can grasp truth and seek wisdom (no. 15); the dignity of the *moral conscience,* which can detect God's law within (no. 16); the dignity of the *will,* which is free to choose good or evil. We will examine some of these aspects of human dignity in more detail, since they are foundational to the Catholic understanding of the person in the modern world.

What do we mean by "conscience"?

The constitution calls conscience a person's "most secret core and sanctuary," where he "detects a law which he does not impose upon himself, but which holds him to obedience. Always summoning him to love good and avoid evil, the of conscience can when necessary speak to his heart more specifically; do this, shun that. For man has in his heart a law written by God. To obey it is the very dignity of man; according to it he will be judged" (no. 16).

Conscience guides all people to "objective norms of morality" that have God as their source, and which are "fulfilled by love of God and neighbor" (no. 16). Everyone, Christians and non-Christians alike, are bound to follow the dictates of their conscience.

However, part of human dignity is to seek to *form* our consciences by seeking truth and goodness. Can conscience err? Yes, but God does not condemn us for this error if we are genuinely seeking the truth. "The same cannot be said of a man who cares but little for truth and goodness, or of a conscience which by degrees grows practically sightless as a result of habitual sin" (no. 16).

Do people really possess "free will"?

Despite the contentions of some behavioral scientists and the Calvinistic view that all things are determined by God, the Catholic church continues to teach that the human person possesses authentic freedom of choice. The pastoral constitution explains that there can be no real human goodness without genuine freedom to choose the good. This freedom is a sign of the image of God in each man and woman. In sum, "man's dignity demands that he act according to a knowing and free choice" (no. 17).

Normally the greatest limitation on the freedom of a person is due to sin, which blinds us and inhibits our ability to freely choose the good. Only with the help of God's grace can freedom be restored and exercised fully. Because we are truly free, each person is responsible for his or her own decisions and actions. "Before the judgment seat of God each man must render an account of his own life, whether he has done good or evil" (no. 17, see 2 Cor 5:10).

It seems to me that this *responsibility* that flows from human freedom is very important to understanding the church in the modern world today. Many modern people are not taught to take responsibility for their actions, to accept the responsibility that goes with freedom. We desire freedom, but will we take responsibility for the effects of our free choices and actions? Any parent knows that as their children grow they desire greater freedom to choose and act. But they must be taught to take responsibility for their choices and to accept the consequences of them, for good or ill.

Why do we have to suffer?

The Council views the suffering of the world largely as a result of humankind's own free choices based upon sin (no. 13), not something inflicted by our good Creator. Death is a mystery that presents the greatest challenge to human existence. Far from evading the question of death, Christianity faces it squarely and answers that death is the result of sin. "Man has been created by God for a blissful purpose beyond the reach of earthly misery." Jesus Christ has won the victory over death when he rose to life, "since by His death He freed man from death" (no. 18).

Given the reality of suffering, is atheism a more realistic belief than Christianity? Atheism cannot explain suffering and death, because it supposes there is no goal or meaning to life other than that which we create. Christians believe that suffering and death have a purpose in God's plan that can be discovered. The ultimate question is not whether atheism or Christianity is more attractive or "realistic," but which view is correct, is *true*.

The constitution acknowledges that Christians whose faith is weak or in error, or whose conduct contradicts their faith, can cause Christianity to appear untrue or less desirable than atheism or other religious systems when faced with the mystery of death. Nonetheless, the church strongly rejects atheism and proposes that the best response to atheism is a proper presentation of the church's teaching and the authentic life of the church and her members. "What does the most to reveal God's presence, however, is the brotherly charity of the faithful who are united in spirit . . . and who prove themselves a sign of unity" (no. 21).

The church professes that all people must work together for the betterment of the world in which we all live. While working prudently with atheists, the church "courteously invites atheists to examine the gospel of Christ with an open mind." The message of the gospel is in harmony with the deepest desires of the human heart. Far from diminishing man, it "brings to his development light, life, and freedom" (no. 21). As St. Augustine wrote after many years of searching for God "You have made us for yourself, O Lord, and our hearts are restless until they rest in you" (*Confessions* 1:1).

What is the ultimate key to understanding the human person?

Jesus Christ. "The truth is that only in the mystery of the incarnate Word does the mystery of man take on light" (no. 22). The first part of *The Pastoral Constitution on the Church in the Modern World* is so structured that the end of each chapter explains how Jesus Christ is the ultimate answer and key to understanding the mystery of the human person (ch. 1), the communal nature of humanity (ch. 2), human activity in the world (ch. 3), and the role of the church in the modern world (ch. 4). Thus the whole constitution is Christocentric, centered on the person and work of Jesus Christ, who is the "new man"—the model and goal of redeemed humanity.

Don't we need to avoid a false "individualism"?

The Pastoral Constitution on the Church in the Modern World noted that one of the most striking features of the modern world is that people are increasingly recognizing their interdependence—how the actions of a part of the world's peoples often affect the whole world, for good or ill (no. 23).

The constitution points out that this reality is rooted in God's plan for the human race. God wills that we live together in society in order to lead each other to salvation. God's law governing all of human interaction can be boiled down to this: "Thou shalt love thy neighbor as thyself" (Rom 13:9-10, cf. 1 Jn 4:20).

The basic message of the gospel speaks of God saving us as a people (not merely as individuals), and stresses that this salvation depends on how we treat and relate to one another. Hence, Catholics cannot understand their lives and salvation in a purely individualistic manner. God has joined us together in human society and in the church in order that we might love and serve each other, and thus attain salvation together.

Does society exist for the good of the person?

Yes. Because the individual person is a social being, created by God to live in society, Catholics insist that the good of the person and of society as a whole are interrelated. In terms of priority, however, "the subject and goal of all social institutions is and must be the human person, which for its part and by its very nature stands completely in need of social life" (no. 25).

Social life is essential to human nature, yet society exists for the good of the person, and not vice versa. Catholics, therefore, must reject Marxism and any view of society which claims that the individual ultimately exists for the good of the state, as a replaceable "cog" in the great all-important "machine" of human society.

Some social entities are absolutely essential for human welfare, such as the family and the political community. Other social groups originate and develop from the free decision of the person. All of these social groups have a great impact on forming the persons who belong to them.

Shouldn't individuals and social groups promote the "common good"?

The constitution acknowledges that individuals and groups "must take account of the needs and legitimate aspirations of other groups, and even of the general welfare of the entire human family" (no. 26). Yet the constitution insists that the "common good" cannot be in violation of the basic rights and dignity of the human person "since he stands above all things, and his rights and duties are universal and inviolable" (no. 26).

You cannot, for example, destroy innocent human life in order to advance or protect the "quality of life" or the "common good" of other persons. If the lives of some innocent persons are threatened, then *everyone* in society is endangered, at least in principle, and the common good is thereby hindered, and not advanced.

The constitution concludes that the social order must always work to the benefit of the human person "...and not contrariwise, as the Lord indicated when He said that the Sabbath was made for man, and not man for the Sabbath" (no. 26).

What are the rights of each person?

The Council explicitly lists the following:

- "everything necessary for leading a life truly human, such as food, clothing, and shelter;
- the right to choose a state of life freely and to found a family;
- the right to education;
- to employment;
- to a good reputation;
- to respect;
- to appropriate information;
- to activity in accord with the upright norm of one's own conscience;

- to protection of privacy;
- to rightful freedom in matters religious . . ." (no. 26).

Are certain practices condemned that are opposed to human life and dignity?

Yes. One of the strongest and most explicit renunciations of evil contained in *any* Catholic conciliar document is found in *The Pastoral Constitution on the Church in the Modern World:*

> Furthermore, whatever is opposed to life itself, such as any type of murder, genocide, abortion, euthanasia, or willful self-destruction, whatever violates the integrity of the human person, such as mutilation, torments inflicted on body or mind, attempts to coerce the will itself; whatever insults human dignity, such as subhuman living conditions, arbitrary imprisonment, deportation, slavery, prostitution, the selling of women and children; as well as disgraceful working conditions, where men are treated as mere tools for profit, rather than as free and responsible persons; all these things and others of their like are infamies indeed. They poison human society, but they do more harm to those who practice them than those who suffer from the injury. Moreover, they are a supreme dishonor to the Creator. (no. 27)

Note that in the moral order, the constitution says that these crimes harm the perpetrators more than the victims. The innocent victims will suffer pain or even physical death in this life. But, unless they repent, those who willfully carry out these crimes (knowing that they are evil either through the church's teaching or their own conscience), become hardened and less human in this life. Such persons will suffer the just punishment of God for their sin after death.

How should we treat those who commit such evil acts?

Rather than judging them or returning evil for evil, the constitution urges Catholics to: "speak the saving truth to all men," to those who practice evil, and to ". . . distinguish between error, which always merits repudiation, and the person in error, who never loses the dignity of being a person, even when he is flawed by false or inadequate religious notions. God alone is the judge and searcher of hearts; for that reason He forbids us to make judgments about the internal guilt of anyone" (no. 28).

In other words, we can judge the action as evil, but not the person. We must hate the sin, but love the sinner. We must forgive, even our enemies and those who persecute us. That is what is distinctive about being a follower of Christ: "The teaching of Christ even requires that we forgive injuries, and extends the law of love to include every enemy, according to the command of the New Law: 'You have heard that it was said, "Thou shalt love thy neighbor, and shalt hate thy enemy." But I say to you, love your enemies, do good to those who hate you, and pray for those who persecute and calumniate you' (Mt 5:43-44)" (no. 28).

Are there any other "social sins" that are condemned?

This document asserts the basic equality of all people and states that "every type of discrimination, whether social or cultural, whether based on sex, race, color, social condition, language, or religion, is to be overcome and eradicated as contrary to God's intent" (no. 29). An example is given of "a woman who is denied the right and freedom to choose a husband, to embrace a state of life, or to acquire an education or cultural benefits equal to those recognized for men" (no. 29). Some Catholics may not be aware that the Second

Vatican Council spoke out so strongly to procure these basic rights for women!

Isn't such a view of social responsibility challenging?

Yes. The constitution exhorts Catholics to break from "a merely individualistic morality." Instead we are to consider it a "sacred obligation to count social necessities among the primary duties of modern man, and to pay heed to them" (no. 30).

This document notes how easy it is to ignore the needs of others around us, to be "drugged by laziness," and hence fail to contribute to the common good of society and of other people according to our resources and abilities. There are also those who profess "grand and rather noble sentiments," but "nevertheless in reality live always as if they cared nothing for the needs of society" (no. 30). Can any of us identify with these failings? (I can!) One can have great aspirations to serve or to give money, but just never get around to doing it.

The call is for *participation* by Catholics in the life of society for the good of others. We must overcome obstacles such as poverty (which can focus people almost exclusively on their own needs) or affluence by which a person ". . . indulges in too many of life's comforts and imprisons himself in a kind of splendid isolation" (no. 31). The constitution also praises those nations whose policies ". . . allow the largest number of citizens to participate in public affairs with genuine freedom" (no. 31). My mother, for example, was involved for years with the League of Women Voters, which encouraged citizens to vote and to become more knowledgeable about public affairs.

"God did not create man for life in isolation, but for the formation of social unity" (no. 32). This truth is demonstrated most fully in Jesus Christ, who took flesh in order to share in our human condition, who preached the necessity of treating one another as brothers, and who founded "a new brotherly community," the church, in which we might learn how we should love one another as he has loved us. Our responsibilities as members of the "global community" should first be shown and practiced by how we conduct ourselves and relate as members of the "community of Jesus Christ," the church (no. 32).

How does the church look upon human efforts to shape the world?

The third chapter of *The Pastoral Constitution on the Church in the Modern World* is devoted to discussing human activity in the world. Some major points include that Christians do not see any necessary opposition between human activity and God's power and freedom. Rather we are "... convinced that the triumphs of the human race are a sign of God's greatness ..." (no. 34). In fact, Christians are bound by the gospel to build up the world and to care for the needs of others through our activity.

Yet the greatest value of human activity, as we have noted, is not that a person alters things and society, but that the person develops himself or herself. "A man is more precious for what he *is* than for what he *has*" [or *"does"*] (no. 35, emphasis mine). Constructive activity enhances and promotes the dignity of the person who performs it.

This is a major theme of Pope John Paul II's encyclical letter, *On Human Work (**Laborem Exercens**)*, issued September 14, 1981. The Pope writes, "The Christian vision of reality focuses on man and his dignity as a person created in God's image." This means that the person is the first priority in work; that work is for the person and not the person for work. (This is a hard saying for "workaholics" and those constantly working just to "get ahead.") The final goal of any kind of work is always the benefit of the person.

Thus, the Holy Father concludes: ". . . Man is the axis

around which the entire organization of work must move. Work is a great thing. But man is incomparably greater. Man is sacred. And this sacredness is inviolable" (**LE**, no. 6)

The pastoral constitution summarizes that the norm of human activity is 1.) to promote the genuine good of the human race according to God's plan, and 2.) that it should enable people to pursue and fulfill the vocation that God has given them, so that they may live a truly human life.

Who best exemplifies the meaning and dignity of work?

We see the dignity of work in Jesus, who was born into the home of a carpenter and himself worked in his father's trade until age thirty, when he began his public ministry of preaching and teaching about the kingdom of God. The Son of God was both a skilled laborer and a teacher.

His mother, Mary, the most exalted of all women, spent her days making a home and caring for her family and later for the church. Her ministry, too, was one of work in the home, prayer, and service to God's people.

Could combining work and religion threaten the rightful independence of human affairs and science?

The pastoral constitution speaks of the "autonomy of earthly affairs," which means that God has created things to exist and to operate with "their own stability, truth, goodness, proper laws, and order" (no. 36). Religion does not interfere with methodical investigations which seek to understand how and why things exist and work as they do. There is then, no such thing as "Christian chemistry" or "Christian physics" per se, except that a Christian may apply and implement his or her findings in a different way than others, according to authentic moral standards.

The "autonomy of earthly affairs" does *not* mean that "created things do not depend on God, and that man can use them without any reference to their Creator'' (no. 36). To the contrary, understanding how things and people are made by God can show us that they have proper and improper uses and behavior. A true understanding of people and things can even lead individuals to discover God, as he is manifest in his works (see Rom 1:19, 20).

Is there a "dark side" to human activity and progress?

Yes. The pastoral constitution recognizes human activity is also caught up into that "monumental struggle against the powers of darkness [which] pervades the whole history of man'' (no. 37). This war began at the origin of the world and will continue until the end of history, at the day of Christ's return in glory (no. 37).

Although human progress *can* serve the true happiness of humanity, it has also been infected and corrupted by sin: "Hence if anyone wants to know how this unhappy situation can be overcome, Christians will tell him that all human activity, constantly imperiled by man's pride and deranged self-love, must be purified and perfected by the power of Christ's cross and resurrection'' (no. 37).

All human activity reaches its perfection through the power of God present in the paschal mystery of Christ's passion, death, and resurrection. Through the work of the Holy Spirit, God purifies our activity from sin, gives us a vision of God's will, and arouses a desire for the age to come when all sin will be wiped away. Only then will all our human activity and achievements be brought to perfection in Christ.

Is it possible to build the kingdom of God on earth?

This constitution states, "Earthly progress must be carefully distinguished from the growth of Christ's kingdom. Nevertheless, to the extent that the former [earthly progress] can contribute to the better ordering of human society, it is of vital concern to the kingdom of God" (no. 39). In short, people cannot directly build Christ's kingdom, but we can cooperate with God's work of establishing his kingdom by ordering society according to God's will and plan. For example, working through political means to establish a just society does not bring about the kingdom of God. Even if that just society were attained perfectly, the kingdom of God in its fullness is always greater and more magnificent than anything we could accomplish on earth. However, a just society would be a sign of God's reign that can hasten the coming of God's kingdom, and is a fulfillment of the Lord's prayer, "...thy kingdom come, thy will be done on earth as it is in heaven."

How would you summarize the relationship between the church and the world?

The church is in the world, and so experiences everything that is common to humanity. Thus the church and the world penetrate each other. There are various ways that the church can serve the world, and in which the world can contribute to the church. The church can feed the poor, encourage constructive scientific research, promote justice and peace, and, most importantly, tell the world the meaning and purpose of human existence. The world contributes to the church the richness of its diverse cultures, its endeavors and findings that promote the welfare of humanity, and various means of spreading the gospel of Jesus Christ more effectively, such as through the modern mass media. The relationship between the church and the world is like a soul to a body, as the "Letter to Diognetius" observed in the second century. This document also states that the church is "a leaven and...a kind of soul for human society, as it is to be renewed in Christ and transformed into God's family" (no. 40).

How does the church serve individuals?

The church primarily serves individuals by shedding light on the meaning of their existence and proclaiming that only God meets and fulfills the deepest longing of the human heart. The church also proclaims and seeks to safeguard the dignity and value of each human person (no. 41), as we see in her efforts against human rights violations, poverty, social injustice, abortion, infanticide, euthanasia, and so on.

How does the church serve society?

"Christ, to be sure, gave His Church no proper mission in the political, economic, or social order. The purpose which He set before her is a religious one" (**GS**, no. 42). However, the religious mission of the church provides a light and energy for human society that can help us live together according to the law of God. God's law ultimately applies to all human life and relationships, including social, political, and economic realms. For instance, all people of good conscience recognize the value of peace among peoples and nations based upon justice, forthright mutual agreements, and reconciliation where needed. These are all aspects of God's will and his law.

The church is also to be a model and source of *unity* for the world. Because the church is not identified with any particular culture or social system, she is able to bring together different human communities and nations.

How does the church contribute to human activity?

A hallmark of the Second Vatican Council is the teaching of this constitution that Christians cannot shirk their earthly responsibilities because they are seeking a heavenly kingdom. The pastoral constitution declares that the "split between the faith which many profess and their daily lives deserves to be counted among the more serious errors of our age" (no. 43). There is to be no false dichotomy between activity and life in society and religious life. The constitution even goes so far to state that, "The Christian who neglects his temporal duties neglects his duties toward his neighbor and even God, and jeopardizes his eternal salvation" (no. 43).

A strong statement! Being a Christian does not only include "religious activities," but means engaging in a Christ-like manner in fulfilling one's duties in the affairs of the world. The constitution proceeds to discuss the role of lay people, whose main arena of activity is the world. Bishops, priests, and others set apart for the religious service should also be concerned about how their lives witness to Christ's presence in the world.

Hasn't the church fallen short of fulfilling this mission?

The pastoral constitution honestly admits that "among her members, both clerical and lay, some have been unfaithful to the Spirit of God during the course of many centuries. In the present age, too, it does not escape the Church how great a distance lies between the message she offers and the human failings of those to whom the gospel is entrusted" (no. 43).

This document encourages Catholics to be aware of those failings and to work to correct them, if presently existing. Also it speaks of a "ripening which comes with the experience of centuries," by which the church is growing in her understanding of God's will and the proper relationship between the church and society. We do not have all the answers, but we trust that the Holy Spirit will continue to guide the church into all truth.

Does the church have anything to gain from the world?

Another major advance of Vatican II is the recognition of all that the church has gained and learned from the history of humanity. For example, the church is indebted to the "ideas and terminology of various peoples" in expressing the message of Christ, as well as to the "wisdom of philosophers" in understanding and clarifying this message such as the Greek philosophical expression *homoousios* used to define clearly Christ's full divinity (**GS**, no. 44).

Nonetheless, all that the modern world has to offer to the church must be discerned by the help of the Holy Spirit. A crucial task of the entire people of God, especially pastors and theologians, is "to hear, distinguish, and *interpret* the many voices of our age and to judge them in light of the divine Word" (**GS**, no. 44, emphasis mine).

This discernment of what is good and helpful from our age, and what is harmful to or incompatible with Christian faith, remains one of the greatest challenges to Christians in relationship to the modern world. In the final chapter of this book, for example, we will discuss the need for discernment in using the "mass media." Good and evil are certainly admixed to a striking degree in this area, as they are in other areas of business, politics, and commerce, to name a few.

What then is the goal of the church in relationship to the modern world?

The heart of the Catholic challenge of the church in the modern world is "to unite all things in him, things in heaven and things on earth" (Eph 1:10). We wish to exalt Jesus Christ, the light of the world, the alpha and the omega. In the words of the constitution: "the Church has a single intention: that God's kingdom may come, and that the salvation of the whole human race may come to pass. . . . The Lord is the goal of human history, the focal point of the longings of history and of civilization, the center of the human race, the joy of every heart, and the answer to all its yearnings" (no. 45).

This chapter has examined the principles for under-standing the life and mission of the church in the modern world. The next chapter will explore some specific challenges that confront the church in the world today.

RECOMMENDED READING

The Pastoral Constitution on the Church in the Modern World (***Gaudium et Spes***), Introduction and Part I. Abbott ed., pp. 199-248; Flannery ed., pp. 903-947.

QUESTIONS FOR GROUP DISCUSSION

1. Looking at the world situation can easily lead to hopelessness or pessimism. How should Catholics view the condition of the world today?

2. How is the Catholic understanding of the world based on understanding the nature of the human person and humanity's relationship with God? Why is the Catholic belief in the dignity of each person so essential to all Catholic social teaching? Discuss.

3. What forms of atheism do we encounter in the world? What can we do about this atheism?

4. What is the Catholic understanding of the purpose of society? What are some practices or beliefs that contradict society's true purpose in God's plan? Discuss.

5. What does the Catholic church teach about the purpose and value of work? Is Christianity opposed to progress, science, or other things that have the potential to serve people's needs?

6. What does the Catholic church have to contribute to modern society through its teaching and the activity of its members? What can we learn from modern society? How is Jesus Christ the ultimate answer to the needs and concerns of this age?

PERSONAL CHALLENGE

Most people find it difficult to find time and energy to become very involved in public life. Yet normal daily activity often puts us in contact with others who have needs and concerns, joys and griefs. This constitution challenges us to open our eyes to the world around us—to sharpen our understanding of the way Catholics view the human person, society, work, and the modern world in general.

Ask yourself: Does my faith in Christ enable me to view the condition of the modern world with hope, in spite of all the problems I see? Do I understand that the sorry condition of the world is due in large part to humanity's sin and rebellion against God and his plan for human life (and do I see how my own rebellion contributes to them)?

Am I familiar with authentic Catholic teaching about the dignity of the human person, the purpose of society and human activity, and the church's mission in the world? Would further study or reflection help me to understand better the basic Catholic teaching in any of these areas?

Do I see my work, service in the world, and other daily activities as separated from (or even opposed to) my spiritual life and religious concerns and activities? How can I come to see them more clearly related as all part of God's purpose and will for my life? How is God calling me to think and act in order to further the church's essential mission in the world?

RESOURCE LIST

On Human Work, (***Laborem Exercens***), Pope John Paul II.

On the Social Concern of the Church, (***Sollicitudo Rei Socialis***), (December 30, 1987), Pope John Paul II.

Catholic Social Teaching: Our Best Kept Secret, P.J. Henriot, E.P. De Berri, M.J. Schultheis (New York: Orbis, 1985).

The Social Teaching of Vatican II, Rodger Charles, S.J., with Drosten Maclaren, O.P. (San Francisco: Ignatius Press, 1982).

The Way of the Lord Jesus, A Summary of Catholic Moral Theology, Vols. I and II, Germain Grisez (Chicago, IL: Franciscan Herald Press, 1983).

All of the modern papal social encyclicals, beginning with Pope Leo XIII's ***Rerum Novarum,*** 1891.

FIVE

Specific Challenges Confronting the Church in the Modern World

D OES CHRISTIANITY, and the Catholic church in particular, address the really "tough" issues that fill the media and the ones that we encounter personally every day? What does the church have to say about the pain of divorce and the break-up of families? About the disintegration of Christian culture in the West and the great diversity of other cultures that influence us in our "global village"? About politics and economics as we face difficult choices and the stark reality of hunger and poverty all around us? And how do we even begin to attain and maintain peace in a world lapsing continually into war and conflict?

While the first part of *The Pastoral Constitution on the Church in the Modern World* (*Gaudium et spes*) presented some foundational principles for a Catholic's approach to the modern world, this second part confronts these urgent issues with some direct and practical applications of these principles.

One important goal of the Second Vatican Council was to put the Catholic church in touch with modern needs and problems. The Extraordinary Synod of 1985 clarified that bringing the church "up-to-date" (*aggiornamento*) does not mean "an easy accommodation [to the modern world] that could lead to the secularization of the Church," but rather calls Catholics to "a missionary openness for the integral salvation of the world." "Integral salvation" means that Catholics defend all truly human values, (such as the dignity of the human person; fundamental human rights; peace; freedom from oppression, poverty and injustice), while realizing that these efforts must be "further elevated through grace" and lead to "familiarity with God, through Jesus Christ, in the Holy Spirit" (**ES**, p. 63). In other words, the church does not promote authentic human values as a social program carried out by purely human efforts, but seeks to promote these values through the power and guidance of God in order to lead the world ultimately to the fullness of salvation in Jesus Christ and in his Holy Spirit.

Let us, then, examine how this document speaks of the salvific work of the church in these important areas of modern life.

How does the Catholic Church view marriage in the modern world?

This pastoral constitution recalls the basic reasons why marriage was instituted by God and confirmed by Jesus Christ as a sacrament of the church. These are, first, for the good of the spouses through the mutual giving of their whole selves to each other (conjugal love), and secondly for the proceation and education of children, which is a main purpose and even the "ultimate crown" of marriage and conjugal love (no. 48). The constitution states clearly that "children are really the supreme gift of marriage ..." (no. 50).

The constitution teaches that "authentic married love is caught up into divine love and is governed and enriched by

Christ's redeeming power and the saving activity of the Church" (no. 48). Married love cannot survive and flourish without the grace of God given through Christ and his church. "For this reason, Christian spouses have a special sacrament by which they are fortified . . ." to live their married lives fully and faithfully (no. 48).

The need for this sacramental grace is especially evident in the West, where traditional social supports to the unbreakable bond of marriage are rapidly disappearing. It becomes increasingly difficult to live "total fidelity" and to grow into deeper unity day by day, even among those who recognize the importance of this both for the good of their spouse and for their children.

In sum, the Second Vatican Council reaffirms the sanctity of marriage and the indissolubility of a true Christian marriage. It points to the grace of the sacrament of matrimony as sufficient and necessary to preserve the couple's conjugal love and unity, and to strengthen the couple for the bearing and rearing children.

What does Vatican II say about the responsibility of Christian parents to have children?

Children are a gift of God. This pastoral constitution affirms that although there are other purposes of marriage, the bearing and raising of children is the proper mission and task of Christian couples by which they cooperate with the love of God the Creator.

In determining how children should be added to the family, the constitution calls for "human and Christian responsibility" based on reverence toward God and his law (as presented by the church's teaching office) and with consideration of the material and spiritual conditions of the times and the family. In other words, the regulation of birth is a matter of conscience, but ". . . a conscience dutifully conformed to the divine law itself, and . . . submissive toward the Church's teaching office, . . ." (no. 50). In article 51, the pastoral constitution provides a brief preliminary outline of the reasons behind the Catholic church's teaching on the regulation of birth that are explained more fully in Pope Paul VI's encyclical letter of 1968, *On the Regulation of Birth* (*Humanae Vitae*). The Catholic church accepts only natural means of birth regulation that do not artificially obstruct or interfere with the normal sexual process of reproduction. As the document states beautifully, ". . . the acts themselves which are proper to conjugal [married] love and which are exercised in accord with genuine human dignity must be honored with great reverence" (no. 51).

This teaching is based on the presupposition "that human life and the task of transmitting it are not realities bound up with this world alone" (no. 51). Human beings are not the creators of human life. At best, they are cooperators with God in his plan for the life and destiny of persons. For this same reason, the Catholic church demands that "from the moment of its conception life must be guarded with the greatest care, while abortion and infanticide are unspeakable crimes" (no. 51).

The constitution readily points out that even couples who are unable to have children can experience the beautiful gift of mutual love, support, and communion in marriage (no. 50). Nonetheless, this document makes "special mention" of couples who have chosen, with wise deliberation and gallant hearts to bring up "even a relatively large family" (no. 50). The large family is still praiseworthy in the eyes of the Catholic church!

What does Vatican II say about the role and importance of the family in the modern world?

The Pastoral Constitution on the Church in the Modern World calls the family "the foundation of society" and a "school of deeper humanity" (no. 52). However, the family will only succeed in leading members to deeper humanity if the family *prays* together; if the parents *educate* their children (especially religious education) and give a good example (no. 48); if the father is *actively present* in their formation, and the children, especially the younger ones, receive the care of the mother at home (no. 52); if the mother's *domestic* role is preserved and respected, "though the legitimate social progress of women should not be underrated on that account" (no. 52).

The children, too, contribute to the family by obeying their parents and responding to their parents' kindness "with sentiments of gratitude, with love and trust" and standing by their parents in hardship and old age (no. 48).

Preserving and rebuilding marriage and family life is a high priority for the whole of society today. The constitution insists, "Public authority should regard it as a sacred duty to recognize, protect, and promote their authentic nature, to shield public morality, and to favor the prosperity of domestic life. The right of parents to beget and educate their children in the bosom of the family must be safeguarded" (no. 52).

Obviously, there is much work to be done here. In his apostolic exhortation, *On the Role of the Christian Family in the Modern World* (**Familiaris Consortio**), Pope John Paul II gives further guidelines and helps for Catholics and others who are concerned for the preservation and restoration of marriage and family life as a firm foundation of human society.

What does the church have to say about the proper development of culture?

Culture is something that affects our daily lives, personalities, and living environments. Unfortunately, there are elements of any world culture that do not promote full human existence and dignity. In the West, for example, we live in a culture that supports egocentrism, materialism, and hedonism. It promotes a life that is centered on self, money and possessions, enjoyment, and sex. Wherever they live, Catholics must become aware of both the positive and negative elements of their cultural environment.

The second chapter of part two of this constitution encourages Catholics to form culture according to true human and Christian values. While it does form each of us, culture is first to be formed by the men and women of the society. *We* are the creators of culture!

This constitution notes that we are in an historical period in which new forms of culture are emerging because of a more unified world, the advances of science and technology, and a growing common awareness of humanity's responsibility to build a better world based upon truth and justice (no. 56).

How does our Catholic faith affect our role in the development of culture?

Christians are on a pilgrimage toward a heavenly city. This *increases* the weight of our responsibility to work with others in constructing a more human world (no. 57). Through the incarnation of his Son, we know that God takes seriously the affairs and transformation of the world. We will be judged according to how we live in the world. Catholics are to oppose elements of culture that contradict the truths that we know by faith, such as the belief that science or reason are the *only* means of discovering the truth. The church is not bound to any one culture. She seeks to confirm and purify the truth to be found in any cultural expression. The constitution summarizes the approach of Catholics to culture:

The good news of Christ constantly renews the life and culture of fallen man. It combats and removes the errors and evils resulting from sinful allurements which are a perpetual threat. It never ceases to purify and elevate the morality of peoples. By riches coming from above, it makes fruitful, as it were from within, the spiritual qualities and gifts of every people and of every age. It strengthens, perfects, and restores them in Christ. Thus by the very fulfillment of her own mission the Church stimulates and advances human and civic culture. By her action, even in its liturgical form, she leads men toward interior liberty. (no. 58)

May the faithful, therefore, live in very close union with the men of their time. Let them strive to understand perfectly their way of thinking and feeling, as expressed in their culture. Let them blend modern science and its theories and the understanding of the most recent discoveries with Christian morality and doctrine. Thus their religious practice and morality can keep pace with their scientific knowledge and with a never-advancing technology. Thus too they will be able to test and interpret all things in a truly Christian spirit. (no. 62)

The Catholic church praises all that is good and true in the cultures of the world, and seeks to purify and perfect these elements by the fullness of truth found in Jesus Christ and his teaching.

What does the church teach about the economic realm?

Scripture warns against the love of money and the serving of money instead of God (1 Tm 6:10; Mt 6:24). Money should serve the dignity and total vocation of the human person, promoting the welfare of societ as a whole. The constitution points out certain abuses, such as money becoming the dominant concern of people's lives in economically advanced areas, and the unjust distribution of wealth which results in the shocking disparity between the comfortable prosperity of a small proportion of the world's population and the grinding poverty of the majority—a contrast which "is becoming more serious day by day" (no. 63). Jesus' parable about the rich man and the beggar, Lazarus, is being realized on a world-wide scale.

What can be done about this situation? *The Pastoral Constitution on the Church in the Modern World* advocates technical and economic development that is directed by, and directed to assist, the greatest number of people. The constitution equally condemns the extremes of capitalism "which obstruct(s) the necessary reforms in the name of a false liberty," and of socialism or communism "which subordinates the basic rights of individual persons and groups to the collective organization of production." Pope John Paul II has taught more fully on the shortcomings of both capitalism and communism in his apostolic letter, *Sollicitudo Rei Socialis.*

What does the constitution have to say about the role of workers?

Workers must be treated as persons and not as mere tools of production (no. 66). Jesus himself illustrated the dignity of work through his own years as a laborer. Those who work must be paid sufficiently to provide for their own material, social, cultural, and spiritual needs, and those of their dependents. Productive work should be adapted to the requirements of a person's life, above all his or her family life (". . . Such is especially the case with respect to mothers of families . . ." no. 67).

What other economic themes are discussed?

In his apostolic letter *On Human Work*, (*Laborem Exercens*), Pope John Paul II has reflected profoundly on the nature and dignity of human work. This pastoral constitution also discusses the right of workers to found labor unions and to participate in the running of business enterprises; the responsibility of management and labor to seek peaceful settlements to disputes; the Christian duty to give to the poor, "and to do so not merely out of their superfluous goods" (no. 69); the investment of money and goods to provide "employment and sufficient income for the people of today and of the future" (no. 70); and the importance of private ownership and private control of material goods so that people can express their personalities and exercise their legitimate role in society and the economy (no. 71).

The position of the Council on the socio-economic realm is summarized by this exhortation from the pastoral constitution:

> Christians who take an active part in modern socio-economic development and defend justice and charity should be convinced that they can make a great contribution to the prosperity of mankind and the peace of the world. Whether they do so as individuals or in association, let their example be a shining one. After acquiring whatever skills and experience are absolutely necessary, they should in faithfulness to Christ and His gospel observe the right order of values in their earthly activities. Thus their whole lives, both individual and social, will be permeated with the spirit of the beatitudes, notably with the spirit of poverty.
>
> Whoever in obedience to Christ seeks first the kingdom of God will as a consequence receive a stronger and purer love for helping all his brothers and for perfecting the work of justice under the inspiration of charity. (no. 72)

Does Vatican II explain the "preferential option for the poor" or the "theology of liberation"?

The Second Vatican Council called attention to the church's mission in service to the poor, the oppressed and the outcast, and urged a prophetic denunciation of every form of poverty and oppression. This denunciation was based on a recognition of the fundamental and inalienable rights of the human person, and included defence of human life "from the time of its very beginning . . ." (**ES**, pp. 65-66).

The "preferential option for the poor" points out the biblical truth that God has a special love and care for the poor. Christians may participate in their own special concern for and service to the poor. The Extraordinary Synod affirmed and praised this preferential option for the poor, but noted that it does not exclude care and concern for those who are not poor, nor is it limited to the alleviation of material poverty to the neglect of spiritual poverty.

The Synod reminds us, "The salvific mission of the Church in relation to the world must be understood as an integral whole. It must involve both the spiritual and the temporal (earthly) needs of mankind." There is certainly a clear distinction—but not a separation—between the natural and the supernatural aspects of the church's mission. The Synod calls Catholics to "put aside the false and useless oppositions between, for example, the Church's spiritual mission and *diaconia* (service) for the world" (**ES**, p. 66).

The "theology of liberation," as taught and practiced over the past twenty-five years, has led to a more careful examination of how the preferential option for the poor is to be properly understood. Clearly the church must oppose unjust and oppressive social structures as part of its service to the poor. But the methods of this opposition must be in accordance with the teaching of Jesus. The spiritual needs of God's people cannot be neglected or seen as less important than human, temporal needs.

In order to clarify the Catholic church's position on the theology of liberation, the Sacred Congregation on the Doctrine of the Faith has issued two instructions, *Instruction on Certain Aspects of the "Theology of Liberation,"* August 6, 1984, and *Instruction on Christian Freedom and Liberation,* March 22, 1986. These may be consulted for further study.

How are Catholics to participate in political life?

The Catholic church is not bound to any political system or party (no. 76). Yet Catholics are to be active in political life in order to safeguard personal rights and promote the common good. The political order exists for the promotion and protection of personal rights such as "the rights of free assembly, of common action, or expressing personal opinions, and of professing a religion both privately and publicly" (no. 73). In fact, these personal rights are necessary conditions for the free and active participation of citizens in government.

Today the recognition is growing of the importance of promoting the rights of *all* citizens, not just a privileged few. The public authority of the political community exists to foster these rights and the common good of all its citizens ". . . exercised within the limits of morality." Citizens are expected to obey public authority, although ". . . it is lawful for them to defend their own rights and those of their fellow citizens against any abuse of this authority, providing that in so doing they observe the limits imposed by natural law and the gospel" (no. 74).

The normal ways that Catholics participate in the political order is by exercising their right to vote, by presenting their views of how the government should be run, by their sense of duty to their country and service to the advancement of the common good, and by serving in political office, a task which the church praises (nos. 75, 76). Christians should be loyal to their countries "but without any narrowing of mind. In other words, they must also look simultaneously to the welfare of the whole human family . . ." (no. 75).

The Catholic church does not place her own hopes in the

privileges conferred by civil authority. She even stands ready to renounce her political rights if their exercise raises doubt about the sincerity of her witness. The duty of the church is "... to preach the faith with true freedom, to teach her social doctrine," and even "... to pass moral judgments, even on matters touching the political order, whenever basic personal rights or the salvation of souls makes such judgments necessary" (no. 76).

The church and its members (especially its politicians) must speak out boldly when basic human rights, or the right to human life itself, is attacked or threatened in any way. There is no distinction made by the Council between one's personal moral beliefs and what one promotes on the political arena. If Christians do not speak out *as Christians*, political communities inevitably will reflect values and pass legislation indifferent or inimical to Christian values, even to the most basic human rights and values. If those who live in democratic political communities are displeased with the legislation passed and judicial decisions being made, we must first ask ourselves whether we have fully accepted the challenge of the Second Vatican Council to actively engage in the political life of our country.

How are efforts toward world peace viewed by the Council?

Christ himself has called his followers to be peacemakers, and declares them "blessed" (Mt 5:9). The constitution focuses on the unification of the world community of nations in the quest for peace. Despite the tremendous obstacles and risks involved, Christians must assume leadership in working for unity and peace in response to Christ's call.

What is peace? How is it to be achieved? The constitution makes its plea for peace founded on a question for justice, "Peace is not merely the absence of war. Nor can it be reduced solely to the maintenance of a balance of power between enemies. Nor is it brought about by dictatorship.

Instead, it is rightly and appropriately called 'an enterprise of justice' (Is 32:7). Peace results from that harmony built into human society by its divine Founder, and actualized by men as they thirst after ever greater justice" (no. 78).

The efforts made for economic equality and full political participation for all, discussed earlier, have significant bearing upon the attainment and maintenance of world peace.

A striking aspect of chapter 5, section one of this constitution is the vehement denunciation of the arms race and of wars that indiscriminately kill combatants and non-combatants alike. Concerning warfare, the constitution declares, "Any act of war aimed indiscriminately at the destruction of entire cities or of extensive areas along with their populations is a crime against God and man himself. It merits unequivocal and unhesitating condemnation" (no. 80).

The arms race is called ". . . an utterly treacherous trap for humanity, and one which injures the poor to an intolerable degree. It is much to be feared that if this race persists, it will eventually spawn all the lethal ruin whose path is now making ready" (no. 81). The Council ultimately urges the banning of all war (no. 82).

What is the path to peace? The Council teaches: "Peace must be born of mutual trust between nations rather than imposed on them through fear of one another's weapons. Hence everyone must labor to put an end at last to the arms race, and to make a true beginning of disarmament, not indeed a unilateral disarmament, but one proceeding at an equal pace according to agreement, and backed up by authentic and workable safeguards" (no. 82).

The constitution also praises those who practice non-violence. It urges governments to protect the rights of those who for reasons of conscience refuse to bear arms, and to provide them with alternative service to the human community (nos. 78, 79).

The closing sections of *The Pastoral Constitution on the*

Church in the Modern World focus on some practical suggestions and approaches to achieve peace: urging citizens of all nations to work for peace with their government officials (no. 82), eliminating primary sources of war such as excessive economic inequalities and the quest for power (*conversion* is needed here!), cooperation between advanced and developing nations, the international coordination and stimulation of economic growth, and the support of organizations promoting such international cooperation and accountability, such as the United Nations. Christians are called and challenged to "collaborate willingly and wholeheartedly in establishing an international order involving genuine respect for all freedoms and amicable brotherhood between all men" (no. 88).

Continuing the tradition of the great Catholic social encyclicals on peace; such as Pope John XXIII's *Peace on Earth* (*Pacem in Terris*), every January 1 the pope addresses the nations on this "World Day of Peace" with a message on this theme. Let us heed and respond to the call of Jesus Christ, the Prince of Peace, as it comes to us through his gospel and the church. Let Christians also pray fervently for peace, as he has urged us to do.

Conclusion

The Pastoral Constitution on the Church in the Modern World outlines many principles governing the church's response to the pressing and urgent needs of the world today. Who will take up these challenges to work for peace, economic justice, political communities guided by human and Christian values, the restoration of culture based upon the dignity and gifts of the person, and the preservation and restoration of married and family life according to God's will?

The lay members of the church are especially called by God to live and work in the world so that it reflects God's truth and values. Our next chapter will explore the essential role of the laity in meeting the Catholic challenge.

Recommended Reading

The Pastoral Constitution on the Church in the Modern World (*Gaudium et spes*), Part II, Abbott ed., pp. 248-308; Flannery ed., pp. 948-1001.

Questions for Group Discussion

1. What is the church's response to the crisis of marriage and family life in the modern world?

2. How can the Catholic church accept the expression of Christianity in various cultures while, at the same time, seeking to transform each culture by the gospel?

1. What are the goals of the Catholic church's mission in regard to work and the economy? Discuss.

4. What does the Council teach about the involvement of the church and its members in politics? What principles should guide Catholics in their political views and activities?

5. How does the Second Vatican Council teach that peace in the world and a stable community of nations might be attained?

Personal Challenge

What is God's personal call to me in each of the areas just discussed? How can I foster marriage and family life according to God's plan? What can I do to bring about the transformation of the culture in which I live so that it might reflect authentic human and moral values? How can I work for the rights of all people to economic justice and to decent and meaningful work for fair pay? Does my participation in the political life of my country contribute to its life and support values pleasing to God? How can I foster peace in the world?

In which of these areas of modern life am I particularly called and equipped to make a contribution? Am I willing to prayerfully consider or reconsider my responsibilities toward God and my fellow human beings in these areas?

RESOURCE LIST

A Call To Families: Study Guide and Commentary for **Familiaris Consortio**, John S. Hamlon (Collegeville, MN: Human Life Center, 1984).

Covenant of Love, Pope John Paul II on Sexuality, Marriage and Family in the Modern World, Richard Hogan and John LeVoir (New York: Doubleday, 1986).

The Role of the Christian Family in the Modern World (**Familiaris Consortio**), John Paul II.

The Gospel of Peace and Justice, ed. Joseph Gremillion (Maryknoll, NY: Orbis Books, 1976).

On Human Life (**Humanae Vitae**), Pope Paul VI.

Peace on Earth (**Pacem in Terris**), Pope John XXIII.

SIX

The Laity:
A Call to Full Membership
in the Church

A S A LAY CATHOLIC, the call to the laity presented by *The Decree on the Apostolate of the Laity* (**AA**, *Apostolicam actuositatem*) has special meaning for me. It is noteworthy that the first document ever issued by an ecumenical Council that deals solely with the laity should be issued in our lifetime. It is exciting to live in an age in which lay Catholics are being called to assume greater responsibility and leadership in the church and its mission.

By way of example, it is extraordinary that my own lay apostolate simultaneously includes three different areas in my life: my *individual* vocation as a lay theologian in the church; my vocation as a husband and father whose *family* is part of the apostolate and mission of the church; and my vocation to be a part of a predominately lay *association* or *group* of Catholics, The Servants of Christ the King, who are committed to carrying out actively the mission of the church as a community.

Vatican II rightly has been called the "Council of the Laity." As we have seen, the modern world poses a variety of monumental and perilous challenges. God particularly calls the laity to confront these issues and "to seek the kingdom of God by engaging in temporal affairs and by ordering them according to the plan of God" (**LG**, no. 31). To equip lay persons to confront these issues, the Council presents in these documents the beginnings of an official Catholic theology of the laity for modern times.

What are some of the important points of this "lay theology"? First, the Council's focus on the church as "the people of God" makes it clear that the laity, *are* the church, equal in membership with those ordained and vowed to religious life. Each baptized Catholic is as fully a member of the church as the pope. The laity are not "second class citizens" in the church.

Through their baptism and reception of the Eucharist, the lay faithful share fully in the life of Christ and his church. Each lay person has a specific vocation or call from God, a particular way to follow Jesus Christ and to share in the church's life. Each lay person has an "apostolate." He or she is sent out by Christ to carry on his priestly, prophetic, and kingly ministries and to participate in the church's mission in the world in a unique way. Finally, Christ equips lay people with the particular gifts and graces they need to fulfill their vocations and carry out their apostolates successfully.

Catholics have traditionally prayed for vocations to the priesthood and religious life. Now we see the need to pray for vocations to the lay apostolate, as well, so that the world might be more fully and effectively transformed and sanctified from within, as leaven makes a lump of dough rise. As the Council notes, modern conditions demand that the lay apostolate be broadened and intensified and that lay persons carry out their tasks with great zeal.

Due to population growth and scientific and technical progress, there are many places and professional fields— such as in business and science—in which only lay people are capable of making a Christian witness and instilling godly values. Without this witness, there is the real danger of "a certain withdrawal from ethical and religious influences and a serious danger to Christian life" (**AA**, no. 1). However, the Holy Spirit is unmistakeably at work to make the laity ever more conscious of their responsibilities, to inspire them everywhere to serve Christ and the church. Let us now examine some of the aspects of the vocation and apostolate of the laity.

How do lay people carry out Jesus' ministry as priest, prophet, and king?

Priest. As members of God's "royal priesthood" (1 Pt 2:9), lay people offer all their daily work, family life, and other activities to the Father as "spiritual sacrifices acceptable to God through Jesus Christ (cf. 1 Pt 2:5)" (**LG**, no. 34).

Prophet. Catholic lay persons must proclaim Jesus Christ by both *word* and *deed* as prophets of the gospel. The laity "go forth as powerful heralds of faith . . . provided they steadfastly join to their profession of faith a life springing from faith. This evangelization, that is, this announcing of Christ by a living testimony as well as by the spoken word, takes on a specific quality and a special force in that it is carried out in the ordinary surroundings of the world" (**LG**, no. 35).

King. The laity establishes the kingship of Christ first in their own lives, "that by self-denial and a holy life they might conquer the reign of sin in themselves (cf. Rom 6:12)." Second, they bring the kingdom into the lives of others, by leading them, with humility and patience to accept Christ as their king. Third, the laity, guided by a Christian conscience, work to establish God's kingdom and the values of that kingdom in all the affairs of the world, ". . . For even in secular affairs there is no human activity which can be withdrawn from God's dominion. . . ." (**LG**, no. 36).

What do you mean by the word apostolate?

The first chapter of *The Decree on the Apostolate of the Laity* explains that the church was founded to spread the kingdom of Christ everywhere so that the whole world might be brought into relationship with Christ and share in his saving redemption.

The decree says that "it is proper to the layman's state in life for him to spend his days in the midst of the world and of secular transactions; he is called by God to burn with the spirit of Christ and to exercise his apostolate in the world as a kind of leaven" (no. 2).

All activity of the church directed to this goal is called the "apostolate," which is carried on in various ways by all the church's members. The Christian vocation is necessarily a call to the apostolate, a call to carry out the mission of Christ in the world. All lay Catholics receive a common call to share in this mission. Each lay person is called by Christ to exercise his or her own particular lay apostolate, that is, to advance the gospel with the unique gifts and in the area that God has apportioned.

Whenever the decree speaks of the particular way the laity carry out this apostolate, two dimensions are included: first, bringing to all people the message and the grace of Christ that will lead them to holiness; second, renewing the temporal order by "penetrating and perfecting the temporal sphere of things through the spirit of the gospel" (nos. 2 and 5).

How are the laity equipped for this apostolate?

Each lay person is assigned to the apostolate by Jesus Christ himself through baptism, and then strengthened by the power of the Holy Spirit through confirmation. Also "the [other] sacraments, especially the most holy Eucharist, communicate and nourish that charity which is the soul of the entire apostolate. . . ." (**AA**, no. 3).

The Council stresses that it is God's love, poured into our hearts through the Holy Spirit (Rom 5:5), that impels us to promote the spread of God's kingdom so that all will come to know "the only true God and Him whom He sent, Jesus Christ" (cf. Jn 17:3). "On all Christians," the Council declares, "is laid the splendid burden of working to make the divine message of salvation known and accepted by all . . . throughout the world" (no. 3). The laity are equipped for the apostolate since they themselves are filled with the love of Christ and desire to spread the good news about him to everyone. This can be carried out through the apostolate of married and family life, evangelization, political involvement, ecumenical endeavors, and many other expressions of lay involvement aimed at spreading the message of Christ and the advancement of his kingdom.

Doesn't it seem that many Catholics lack this love and zeal?

Yes, and that is why this decree teaches that ". . . the success of the lay apostolate depends upon the laity's living union with Christ. For the Lord has said, 'He who abides in me, and I in him, he bears much fruit: for without me you can do nothing' (Jn 15:5)" (no. 4).

Without a living union with Jesus Christ there is no lay apostolate worth speaking of. Pope John Paul II took this same parable of the vine and the branches as the central theme of his apostolic letter on *The Lay Members of Christ's Faithful People* (**Christifideles Laici,** **CL,** Dec. 30, 1988). He stresses that the fruitfulness and growth of the lay apostolate depends upon the communion or unity of the laity with Jesus Christ. Another way of saying this is that lay people must be holy. As John Paul II states in *The Lay Members of*

Christ's Faithful People, holiness is "a fundamental pre-supposition" and "an irreplaceable condition" for everyone to fulfill the saving mission of the Church. "The Church's holiness is the hidden source and the infallible measure of the works of the apostolate and of the missionary effort. Only in the measure that the Church, Christ's Spouse, is loved by Him and she, in turn, loves Him, does she become a mother fruitful in the Spirit" (**CL**, no. 17). Thus, holiness is absolutely essential in carrying out the lay apostolate.

Is it realistic to expect that lay people can grow in holiness?

It is true that most lay people cannot have the same *type* of spiritual life as priests or religious, but lay people can and must grow in holiness, for this is the call of God to all Christians (see **LG**, chapter 5). *The Decree on the Apostolate of the Laity* mentions some elements of an authentic "lay spirituality" by which lay people can grow in holiness.

First, lay people are "nourished by the spiritual aids which are common to all the faithful, especially active participation in the sacred liturgy" (no. 4). Through the sacraments and other forms of prayer and devotion that are accessible to all, lay people can develop an intimate union with God in prayer.

Second, the decree notes that by fulfilling their normal duties in life according to God's will, lay people grow in union with God and progress in holiness. This includes "trying prudently and patiently to overcome difficulties" (no. 4). "Neither family concerns nor other secular affairs should be excluded from their religious program of life" (no. 4). All things can be done for God and offered to him in thanksgiving (see Col 3:17).

Third, faith and meditation on God's Word enable lay people to seek God's will in all things, and to make correct judgments.

Fourth, the decree affirms that the type of spirituality or

religious life that a lay person pursues will depend on the person's specific state in life, career, vocation, and other factors. The lay person's spiritual life will take its particular form according to whether one is married, widowed, single, and from one's condition of health, profession, social status, and so on. Whatever those may be, the lay person should seek to develop the unique talents God has given and "make use of the gifts which he has received from the Holy Spirit" (no. 4).

How do the gifts of the Holy Spirit equip the laity for their apostolate?

The decree states that the Holy Spirit gives *each* person a charism (gift) or charisms for the building up of the church and the service of humanity. Thus, the lay apostolate is not carried out by human effort or talent alone, but by the exercise of the gifts of the Holy Spirit. "To each is given the manifestation of the Spirit for the common good. To one is given through the Spirit the utterance of wisdom, and to another the utterance of knowledge according to the same Spirit, to another faith by the same Spirit, to another gifts of healing by the one Spirit, to another the working of miracles, to another prophecy, to another the ability to distinguish between spirits, to another various kinds of tongues, to another the interpretation of tongues (1 Cor 12:7-10; cf. 1 Cor 12:4-6, 28-31; Rom 12:6-8; 1 Pt 4:10-11)" (CL, no. 24).

It should be noted that possession of spiritual gifts (and other human talents) is not an indicator of holiness. God gives these gifts freely to whomever he wills for the up-building of the church, not as a mark or sign of the holiness of the individual who possesses the gift. Hopefully, Catholics will use their gifts to give glory to God and to foster their own dedication to Christ, as well as to build up the church.

The pope stresses that the gifts of the Holy Spirit are to be received with gratitude by the individuals who exercise them and by the whole church, since "they are in fact a singularly rich source of grace for the vitality of the apostolate and for the holiness of the whole body of Christ . . ." (**CL**, no. 24). He also notes the need for a continual *discernment of the charisms* by the pastors of the church to see that they are used rightly (**CL**, no. 24).

Both Pope John Paul II and the Vatican II decree on the laity insist that the laity have both a "right and duty" to exercise their charisms ". . . in the Church and in the world for the good of mankind and for the upbuilding of the Church. In so doing, believers need to enjoy the freedom of the Holy Spirit who 'breathes where he wills' (Jn 3:8)" (**AA**, no. 3).

What does Vatican II say about specific "lay ministries"?

Based upon the gifts of the Holy Spirit, there emerge various *ministries* or services (Greek, *diakonia*) for the up-building of the church. Some ministries are recognized and confirmed through ordination to the priesthood or entrance into different types of religious communities or commitments. By virtue of their varied gifts of the Spirit, lay people, too, have ministries in the church.

Some of these, as Pope John Paul II observed, are connected with the church's liturgical celebration, which ". . . is a sacred action not simply of the clergy, but of the entire assembly. It is, therefore, natural that the tasks not proper to the ordained ministers be fulfilled by the lay faithful" (**CL**, no. 23). The pope explains that this also opens the door for lay people to exercise other ministries in the church, including "announcing the word of God and pastoral care" (**CL**, no. 23).

Through the gifts of the Holy Spirit, lay people build up the body of Christ, serve the world, and promote the spread of the gospel and the advance of God's kingdom. In light of this teaching, it should be common for lay people today to be actively exercising these gifts and ministries in the church and in the world, in cooperation with their pastors. The typical Catholic parish has a wide variety of services in which lay people exercise their gifts, including works of mercy (such as the St. Vincent de Paul Society), hospital visitation and visiting the elderly or shut-ins, CCD and service to Catholic schools, extraordinary Eucharistic ministers and lectors, music ministry, and a host of others.

But don't such ministries create tension between lay people and their pastors?

At times. But the point here is not competition or tension, but achieving and recognizing the complementarity between the gifts and ministries of lay people and those of clergy and religious. We are all working together for the same goal—to advance the kingdom of Christ and spread his good news.

Vatican II distinguishes between the ministries of lay people and ordained clergy, noting that these are different ways of sharing in the priesthood of Christ (see **LG**, no. 10; **AA**, no. 2; **CL**, no. 22). "In the Church, there is a diversity of service but unity of purpose" (**AA**, no. 2). Pope John Paul II states that while lay people can fulfill a variety of ministries in the liturgy, in transmitting the faith, and in the pastoral structure of the church, these should be exercised in a way appropriate to lay people which is different from that of the ordained ministers of the church (**CL**, no. 23).

The Dogmatic Constitution on the Church summarizes the mutual expectations that laity and clergy should have. The laity have the right to receive from their pastors the Word of God and the sacraments. Further, the constitution exhorts pastors to "... recognize and promote the dignity as well as the responsibility of the layman in the Church. Let them willingly make use of his prudent advice. Let them confidently assign duties to him in the service of the Church, allowing him freedom and room for action. Further, let them encourage the layman so that he may undertake tasks on his own initiative" (**LG**, no. 37).

Pastors should expect lay people to express their opinions about the church and their needs ". . . in truth, in courage, and in prudence, with reverence and charity . . ." (**LG**, no. 37). Nonetheless, pastors should also expect lay people to *obey* them in their role of teachers and shepherds in the church, and to *pray* for their pastors as those who will have to render an account for their souls (see Heb 13:17). As we can see, the laity are expected to do far *more* in the church than to "pray, pay, and obey!"

Most importantly, laity and clergy are encouraged to get to know each other well and to converse frequently about issues and concerns with the aim of promoting the good of the church (**LG**, no. 37). This mutual cooperation and understanding is an expression of "coresponsibility" of laity and clergy for the life and mission of the church.

What is the unique goal of the lay apostolate?

In cooperation with the pastors and others in the church, Vatican II speaks of a "special obligation" that lay people have to promote the renewal of the temporal order. The things of this world "have been foully abused by serious vices." In our own time, one of these vices is an "idolatry of temporal things," in which the products of modern technology and science have enslaved us instead of serving us. Some people think that they can no longer survive without two cars, microwave ovens, television and radio, a VCR, large freezers, and other modern conveniences.

What sort of renewal is required? The decree declares that the things of this world must be renewed in such a way that they are brought into conformity with the higher principles of Christian life without violating their own proper laws (no. 7), as was explained earlier in the discussion of the legitimate autonomy of temporal things in chapter 4 of this book, *The Catholic Challenge*.

The decree highlights the importance of "Christian social action," which must be carried out according to the principles of *love*, and of justice. While charity is central, the document notes, "The demands of justice should first be satisfied, lest the giving of what is due in justice be represented as the offering of a charitable gift" (no. 8). It must be the goal of Christian social action to see first that justice is being done. Then we should provide charitable help which goes beyond the demands of what is just and right. For example, it is not charity to provide a worker a just wage for his or her labor. Nor is it charity to see that the poor of the world are provided the minimum standards of food, clothing, and shelter. It is only just to provide these things which are abundant elsewhere.

In what fields do lay people carry on their apostolate?

In Pope John Paul II's letter on the laity, he speaks of Jesus' image of the world itself as a field or vineyard in which people are sent to work and harvest. The whole world is the "field" of the lay apostolate!

Everyone is called to work in this field—now! We are in an *urgent* situation: "A new state of affairs today both in the Church and in social, economic, political and cultural life, calls with a particular urgency for the action of the lay faithful. If lack of commitment is always unacceptable, the present time renders it even more so. It *is not permissible for anyone to remain idle*" (**CL**, no. 3, emphasis mine).

The church is also a field of the apostolate in which *all* the laity are called to work and contribute something. In fact, Vatican II warns that "the member who fails to make his proper contribution to the development of the Church must be said to be useful neither to the Church nor to himself" (no. 2).

The decree on the laity lists as the more important fields of action: church communities, especially the parish and the diocese; the family; youth; the social environment; and in national and international affairs.

What about the laity's role in specific fields of the apostolate?

The involvement of the laity in the apostolate should not be narrowly limited to a few areas of the church's life and mission. Lay persons ought to be active "in *every* apostolic and missionary undertaking sponsored by their local parish," and should be ever ready to serve diocesan projects at their bishop's invitation (**AA**, no. 10, emphasis mine).

The lay apostolate in the field of marriage and family life is to be strongly recommended since the majority of adult Catholics are married. The decree teaches that the "supreme task" of the apostolate of Christian couples today is threefold: to manifest ". . . the unbreakable and sacred character of the marriage bond"; "to educate their children in a Christian manner"; to "defend the dignity and lawful independence of the family" (**AA**, no. 11).

The decree proceeds to provide specific guidance for the family apostolate, encouraging the family to pray together both at home and in the liturgical worship of the church, to express mutual affection, to provide hospitality, and to promote justice and good works for the benefit of those in need. Some specific examples of activities that can be carried out by families as their apostolate are listed in the decree: "the adoption of abandoned infants, hospitality to strangers, assistance in the operation of schools, helpful advice and material assistance for adolescents, help to engaged couples in preparing themselves better for marriage, catechetical work, support of married couples and families involved in material and moral crises, help for the aged not only by providing them with the necessities of life, but also by obtaining for them a fair share of the benefits of economic progress" (no. 11).

A whole section (no. 12) is devoted to *youth* and their apostolate. Adults are encouraged to attract young persons to the apostolate by their example and their interest in young people. Pope John Paul II, in his exhortation on the laity, calls youth "the hope of the Church," (CL, nos. 46, 47).

Concerning the social environment, the decree speaks of "the apostolate of the social milieu." This refers to "the effort to infuse a Christian spirit into the mentality, customs, laws, and structures of the community in which a person lives, . . ." This duty especially rests upon the laity since, "it can never be properly performed by others" (no. 13). The lay person can witness most effectively to others who share a common profession, common interests, residence in the same neighborhood, and so on, which the decree calls "the apostolate of like toward like." They testify to Christ not only by their speech, but also by their witness of a life committed to him (no. 13).

What are the methods of accomplishing this apostolate?

The Council speaks of the apostolate carried out by individuals, and by various groups or associations. Every individual Christian is to be a witness to Christ in word and deed and to advance his kingdom through lives of charity. Individual lay persons can often reach places where lay groups and religious cannot. Pope John Paul's letter on the laity speaks of "the absolute necessity of an apostolate carried on by the individual" (CL, no. 28). Unless each Catholic is committed to the apostolate, the mission of the laity as a whole will be weakened or even fail.

However, Vatican II prophetically called for groups of lay people to join together in the apostolate, which reflects the communal nature of the church (**AA**, no. 18). It acknowledged the great variety of lay associations in the apostolate and recommended that "those [associations] which promote and encourage a closer harmony between the everyday life of the members and their faith must be given primary consideration" (no. 19).

Since the Council, there has been such a flourishing of lay associations, groups, communities, and movements that Pope John Paul II speaks of "... a new era of group endeavors of the lay faithful" (**CL**, no. 29). These groups include Communion and Liberation, Focolare, Cursillo, Miles Jesu, Opus Dei, Catholic charismatic prayer groups and covenant communities, and the Apostolate for Family Consecration, to name but a few. These groups are very diverse, "so great is the richness and the versatility of resources that the Holy Spirit nourishes. Yet they have a common purpose: to participate in the Church's mission of carrying forth the gospel of Christ" (**CL**, no. 29).

The Decree on the Apostolate of the Laity affirms that "the laity have the right to found and run such associations and to join those already existing" (no. 19), as long as the associations keep a proper relationship to church authorities. One chapter is largely devoted to explaining how lay people and associations and the Catholic hierarchy may cooperate and maintain good relations.

The apostolic exhortation on *The Lay Members of Christ's Faithful People* expands this teaching and presents some specific criteria for discerning how such associations may be properly formed (**CL**, nos. 29-30). The most important criterion is to look at "the actual fruits" that the group shows in its organizational life and by the work it performs. "You will know them by their fruits" (Mt 7:16).

Pope John Paul II speaks of the power of such groups to transform their surroundings and society. Equally important is the personal support they provide to fellow members in the midst of a secularized world. Such groups can offer

Catholics "a precious help for the Christian life in remaining faithful to the demands of the Gospel and to the commitment to the Church's mission and apostolate" (**CL**, no. 30). For example, many of these groups provide help for their members to pray and to grow spiritually. Yes, we need such mutual support to keep that flame of the spirit of the gospel alive in us!

How are lay people prepared to carry out their mission?

Too often we neglect the formation and training that lay people need to spread the gospel of Christ in the world and to transform human society according to the standard of the gospel. The final chapter of *The Decree on the Apostolate of the Laity* is devoted to discussing formation of lay Catholics for the apostolate.

It is made clear that this formation ". . . takes its special flavor from the distinctively secular quality of the lay state and from its own form of spirituality" (**AA**, no. 29). It is *not* the same as formation for the priesthood or religious life. Some specific characteristics of this formation for the lay apostolate are mentioned.

First, each lay person should be *well-informed* about the modern world and should recognize and develop his or her own human talents and natural abilities. Second, *spiritual formation* is necessary, fostering a life based on strong faith in God and sensitivity to the movement of the Holy Spirit. "This formation should be deemed the basis and condition for every successful apostolate" (**AA**, no. 29). Third, solid *doctrinal instruction* in theology, ethics, and philosophy, according to the situation and ability of each person, is necessary. Fourth, developing *the ability to relate well with people* is valuable, "especially the art of living fraternally with others, cooperating with them, and initiating conversation with them" (no. 29). Finally, the laity must learn "gradually and prudently" to *put all this into practice,* always with a view

toward maturing in Christ and growing in one's understanding of the changing needs of the world.

The last article of *The Decree on the Apostolate of the Laity* (no.
32), speaks of many *aids* that are available to help lay people
acquire this formation. They are all directed towards
developing a deeper knowledge of sacred Scripture and
Catholic doctrine, nourishing a spiritual life, growing in an
appreciation of world conditions, and discovering and
developing suitable methods for service.

When does this training begin?

The decree teaches that training for the apostolate begins
with a child's earliest education, becoming more specific in
adolescence and young adulthood. "The whole of family life,
then, would become a sort of apprenticeship for the
apostolate" (no. 30). Catholic family life is aimed not only at
the Christian education of the young, but at forming
apostles for Jesus Christ! The young must understand that
they are being trained and formed in order to *be sent out* into
the world to spread the good news of Jesus Christ and to
work and pray for the transformation of society according to
Christian values. Parents can foster this by praying and
reading Scripture with their children in the home and
discussing how this actually applies to everyday life. I have
also found that reading and discussing the lives of the saints
with my children often motivates them to want to follow the
Lord and do his will.

Example is another essential part of training for the lay
apostolate. The biography of Catherine de Hueck Doherty,
champion of the poor and foundress of the primarily lay
Madonna House apostolate, relates how Catherine was
prepared for her apostolate to the poor by her parents.
Although the de Huecks belonged to the Russian nobility,
they frequently welcomed the poor into their home and
shared meals with them. This memory deeply impressed
young Catherine and launched her apostolate among the

poor, a story which we find repeated in the lives of many saints.

How are the laity challenged to carry our their apostolate today?

Many directives from *The Decree on the Apostolate of the Laity* are still very current, if not even more important, twenty-five years after the document was issued. The document urges the laity especially to learn sound doctrine on subjects of controversy, and to "provide the witness of an evangelical life in contrast to all forms of materialism" (no. 31).

Lay people should "be instructed in the true meaning and value of temporal things, both in themselves and in their relation to the total fulfillment of the human person" (no. 31). How much we need this instruction, as we are bombarded daily with materialism and other false values that are attached to earthly things by the media and other influences! Christians today are challenged both to monitor their exposure to sources of false values, like movies that promote and glorify sex or violence, and to discuss openly with mature Christians both the truth and the error of what they see and hear in the media. The laity are also encouraged to learn the principles and conclusions of authentic Catholic moral and social teaching, so they will be able to advance this teaching in society and apply it correctly in individual cases.

More recently, Pope John Paul II has challenged the Catholic laity, especially of the "First World," to undertake a great, new effort of "re-evangelization" of their countries and cultures to Christ. He points to rising secularism, materialism or consumerism, atheism, and "indifference to religion and the practice of religion devoid of true meaning," especially among the traditionally Christian countries of Europe and the West, as the reason for this call to re-evangelization. There is a growing number of "unchurched" people in the West who need to hear the good news about

Jesus Christ. Most of these people will never hear the gospel in church. They will hear it, if anywhere, from their fellow Christian acquaintances, co-workers, or friends.

Lay people in the church are being called to carry out their own prophetic mission. First, we are called to evangelize those around us to Christ (even those within our parishes who do not know Christ personally or who fail to follow his teaching faithfully). Second, we are called to influence the broader culture and government toward a renewed belief in God and obedience to him. Hence "evangelization" is becoming a word that Catholics are hearing more frequently from the pope, our bishops, our priests.

But Catholics cannot give to others what they don't have themselves. The lay faithful must be fully alive in Christ, and "know how to put the Gospel and their daily activities of life into a most shining and convincing testimony" (**CL**, no. 34). The "formation of mature ecclesial communities" and a new "systematic work in catechesis"—teaching the faith—are essential in this renewal of the laity.

Once lay Catholics have been formed and renewed in their own faith, they can share that faith effectively with others and apply it to renew the face of the earth.

But lay persons are not alone in this vocation. The whole church, in different ways, contributes to the basic Christian apostolate of leading others to faith and salvation in Jesus Christ, and transforming the world into his image. In the next chapter, we will explore how the Second Vatican Council instructs bishops, priests, and those called to vowed religious life to understand their identity, mission, and apostolate in the modern world.

RECOMMENDED READING

The Decree on the Apostolate of the Laity (**Apostolicam actuositatem**), Abbott ed., pp. 489-521; Flannery ed., pp. 766-798.

QUESTIONS FOR GROUP DISCUSSION

1. Each lay person has a vocation and an apostolate. What are some of the unique characteristics of the lay vocation and apostolate? Discuss.

2. Many lay people still consider themselves unprepared or ill-equipped to carry out an apostolate. How can lay people be stirred up to "burn with the zeal of Christ" and take up the mission of Christ and the church?

3. How can lay people grow in holiness?

4. What fields of lay apostolate are opening up today, either for individuals or through groups or movements? Might any of these fields of the lay apostolate be appropriate for members in your group? Discuss.

5. How can lay people work in unity and cooperation with their pastors? What are some obstacles to this "co-responsibility" that must be overcome?

PERSONAL CHALLENGE

Both the Second Vatican Council and John Paul II have insisted that no lay Catholic can remain idle and fail to respond to Christ's call to spread the gospel and infuse its teaching into the affairs of the world. This summarizes the Catholic challenge to lay people.

Do I understand myself as being called by Jesus Christ in a unique way to live the gospel? How am I being sent by Christ to spread the gospel and transform the world, even if only in a seemingly small way? How could I respond more fully to this call? What am I doing to grow in holiness, realizing that "without faith it is impossible to please [God]" (Heb 11:6)?

Could associating with other individuals or groups help me to carry out my mission as a lay person, or to grow in holiness? What sort of formation, education, or training would be helpful to me now in my particular lay vocation? Where might I seek this?

RESOURCE LIST

The Lay Members of Christ's Faithful People (**Christifideles Laici**), Pope John Paul II (Boston: Daughters of St. Paul, 1989).
In the Midst of Our World: Forces of Spiritual Renewal by Paul Cordes (San Francisco: Ignatius Press, 1988).

SEVEN

The Challenge to Bishops, Priests, and Religious

I N THE AFTERMATH of the Second Vatican Council, the West experienced a dramatic decline in the number of vocations to the priesthood and religious life, as well as numerous priests and religious leaving their ordained ministries and religious vowed life. On the surface, it appeared that priesthood and religious life were experiencing an "identity crisis." Or perhaps the identity proclaimed by the Council was no longer suitable to many present or prospective priests and religious in the West? However, this crisis was not precipitated by the Second Vatican Council so much as by other voices and forces in Western culture that directly undermined priestly and religious life, or seemed to provide attractive alternatives to them.

With regard to bishops, while the Second Vatican Council devoted a great deal of attention to the bishops' collegial role in leading the church, by 1985 the issue of the nature and limits of the bishops' role was raised through controversy over the teaching and governing authority of national episcopal conferences.

Some studies of the Second Vatican Council downplay or overlook the Council's teaching concerning bishops, priests, priestly formation, and religious life. This would be a serious mistake, especially in light of these pressing challenges today. Certainly the basic leadership structure of the Catholic church is not changed by the Council, but a fresh understanding of these roles is presented and a new style or spirit is conveyed which opens the way for renewal among clergy and religious.

While the First Vatican Council focused on the primacy and the infallibility of the pope, the role of bishops, priests, and religious had not been addressed by an ecumenical council since the Council of Trent in the sixteenth century. The time was ripe for a fresh look at these ministries and vocations, especially since Vatican II set out to present a complete, up-to-date understanding of the church, and its life and purpose in the modern world.

If we could put in a nutshell the challenge presented to bishops and priests, some key words would be communion, collegiality, and imitating Christ the Good Shepherd in their pastoral offices. For religious, the challenge is to *re-discover* the call and charisms of their orders, as well as the basic charism and call of religious life, and then to *renew* these charisms in the situation of the modern world, adapting their original call and mission to the context of our own time.

First, let us discuss the concepts of communion, collegiality, and shepherding, as set forth in *The Decree on the Bishops' Pastoral Office in the Church* (**CD**, *Christus Dominus*), *The Decree on the Ministry and Life of Priests* (**PO**, *Presbyterorum ordinis*) and *The Decree on Priestly Formation* (**OT**, *Optatum totius*).

What is the heart of the teaching about bishops and priests?

At the heart of the Council's teaching on bishops and priests and their formation is the concept of "communion," the deep unity and fellowship that believers have in Jesus Christ. The Extraordinary Synod of 1985 called it "the central and fundamental idea of the Council's documents." Communion focuses on our unity in the church—having a common identity, purpose, and mission on earth, even having our eternal destinies bound up with each other. The "communion of saints" does not only refer to the saints in heaven, but also to our communion with them and with each other on earth. The early church speaks of the "koinonia" or close fellowship that Christians share in Christ that was an essential mark of the church from its earlier years. This unity provides the foundation upon which all relationships in the church are to be built. We are truly one in Christ. The sacraments, especially baptism and the Eucharist, provide the grace and power from God for such unity to exist.

The specific way that communion is expressed and lived out among the bishops, including the pope, is through *collegiality*. The secular equivalent of collegiality might be "teamwork" or "team spirit." For example, the bishops are called to show concern for the entire church throughout the world, and not just for their own local churches or dioceses (**CD**, no. 6).

This collaboration among the bishops for the good of the whole church is expressed in many ways: sending of missionaries and funds from one diocese to another which is in need, coordinating together the pastoral journeys of the pope, being involved in the Synod of Bishops and episcopal conferences, cooperating with the world-wide services of the Roman Curia, and so on. The fullest expression of collegial action is found in an ecumenical council, where *all* the bishops gather to decide issues affecting the entire church. Here it is most evident that the bishops work together as a "college" or a "team"—in a communion of faith and love.

How do the bishops work together with the pope?

The pope is a bishop, a member of the college or body of bishops, but he is also its head, just as Peter was both an apostle and the leader of the apostles. The pope represents Christ in a special way as the pastor of all the faithful, as Jesus appointed Peter to shepherd the whole flock of God (see Jn 21:15-19).

The bishops as a body, joined with the pope and never apart from him, share in the care and shepherding of all Christ's faithful people. They serve in the name and person of Christ as the church's primary leaders, priests, and teachers. They faithfully pass on the message of the gospel entrusted to them by the apostles themselves.

The college of bishops can never act as a whole without the pope, since he is the head of this college. The pope is said to have "supreme, full, immediate, and universal authority" over the care of souls (CD, no. 2). Each bishop possesses the "ordinary, proper, and immediate authority" needed to pastor a local church or diocese (CD, no. 8). This means that the bishop is able to freely lead and teach the faithful in his diocese or jurisdiction, but the faithful are also immediately subject to the pope and his teaching as the universal pastor and shepherd of all Christians.

Hence, it is true that the pope has the right and the authority as chief shepherd of the church on earth to pastor directly any situation in the Catholic church in any part of the world. The pope is not overstepping his authority when he intervenes directly in the affairs of any diocese or local church. However, observing the spirit of collegiality, the pope usually works with the bishops in such a way as to strengthen their leadership and to express his communion with them. He observes Jesus' command to Peter to "strengthen your brothers" (Lk 22:32).

What are some ways this communion and collegiality is expressed?

In his pastoral service to the church, the pope makes use of the departments of the Roman Curia, as well as various papal representatives or legates. In response to Vatican II, the Roman Curia has been streamlined and internationalized to better represent the whole church. Also, the Council called for more bishops, especially at the diocesan level, to serve the pope as consultors and in Vatican departments in order to "more adequately apprise the Supreme Pontiff of the thinking, the desires, and the needs of all the churches" (**CD**, no. 10).

A major step toward the collaboration of the pope and the bishops was the establishment of a Synod of Bishops, drawn from the bishops of the world with the charge to meet regularly to discuss specific issues affecting the whole church. They advise the pope of their discernment on important issues of the day. The Synod of Bishops is a specific way in which the bishops share in the responsibility for shepherding the universal church.

Since the close of Council, the popes have held a number of regular Synods, and one Extraordinary Synod of Bishops in 1985 to evaluate and to promote the teaching of the Second Vatican Council. The popes have used the bishops' reports from the regular Synods as the basis for writing "apostolic exhortations" on the topics discussed there.

The pope also meets regularly with groups of bishops from around the world, both on his pastoral journeys to various countries, and when the bishops of different regions travel to Rome to meet with the pope for regularly scheduled *ad limina* visits; these are "state-of-the-diocese" visits, which are made every five years by all bishops with responsibility for their own dioceses.

Isn't there controversy over episcopal conferences?

Episcopal conferences are national or territorial groupings of bishops who meet regularly to pastor and/or discuss issues affecting the church in their countries and to promote the church's apostolate there (**CD**, no. 38). The Council urged that such conferences be established throughout the world and meet together at fixed times, since existing conferences "have furnished outstanding proofs of a more fruitful apostolate" (**CD**, no. 37).

Some questions have arisen, however, concerning the authority, especially the teaching authority, of episcopal conferences. Episcopal conferences in different countries have issued pastoral statements that appear to differ from each other in approach or even in content. For example, the teaching and approach of the U.S. bishops' pastoral letter on war and peace differed significantly from that of the West Germany bishops. How is the unity of the Catholic church's teaching to be preserved? Also what right do individual bishops have to disagree with the decisions or pastoral statements of the episcopal conference to which they belong?

The Catholic church's teaching is fairly clear on the authority of the *whole* college of bishops, and of individual bishops in relationship to the pope and the whole college of bishops. But what about the teaching and pastoral authority of an episcopal conference? Could they sometimes reflect the beliefs of a "national church" on certain issues, rather than those of the universal church?

These questions remain unresolved at this date. The Extraordinary Synod of 1985 stated that ". . . episcopal conferences must keep in mind the good of the Church, that is, the service of unity and the inalienable responsibility of each bishop in relation to the universal Church and the particular church [the pastors]" (**ES**, p. 57). In light of the necessity of these conferences in the pastoral work of the church today, the Synod recommended that their theological "status" should be studied, especially the problem of their doctrinal authority (II, C, 8). This raises that question of how Catholics should respond to pastoral letters and other statements issued by episcopal conferences or their offices. At present, Catholics should view these as an exercise of the ordinary magisterium of the church, which means that they should be heard and responded to with an attitude of respect and willingness to be taught, but *not* as final or infallible statements of church teaching which are beyond improvement or correction on some points.

Does each bishop need to have a concern for the whole church?

Yes. One thing that is evident in *The Decree on the Bishops' Pastoral Office* is the care and sense of responsibility that each bishop has for the universal church. This would even include lands where the Word of God has not yet been proclaimed (no. 6). Therefore, bishops should be ready to promote works of evangelization, to support the missions, and to aid in times of disaster and affliction as they are able.

Even within his own local diocese, the bishop is called to have a pastoral care not only for the Catholics of the diocese, but for *everyone* who lives within that geographical area. Jesus himself expressed care for ". . . sheep, that are not of this fold," and prayed for the day when they would be brought together as "one flock, one shepherd" (Jn 10:16). A bishop's pastoral concern and activity reaches out and extends to others in this way, especially to the poor, the sick, and those most in need.

Far from exalting the merits of bishops or focusing on their privileges, this document is almost exclusively concerned with the duties and responsibilities of bishops, which includes care of some kind for every member of the church and society. A bishop's life is clearly one of sacrificial service—like Jesus Christ's.

What of other aspects of the bishops' pastoral office?

The document on the bishops also discusses how the bishop carries on Jesus' threefold ministry of priest, prophet, and king. The bishop is, above all, a witness to Christ before all (no. 11). In their teaching role, "... a task which is eminent among the chief duties of bishops. They should, in the power of the Spirit, summon men to faith or confirm them in a faith already living" (no. 12). They must present Christian doctrine faithfully, and yet "in a manner adapted to the needs of the times" (no. 13), especially through preaching and catechetical instruction. This instruction, which includes a new emphasis on the instruction of adult catechumens (RCIA), "is based on sacred Scripture, tradition, the liturgy, the teaching authority and life of the Church" (no. 14).

In their priestly role, "Bishops enjoy the fullness of the sacrament of orders, and all priests as well as deacons are dependent upon them in the exercise of authority" (no. 15). To express this, the bishop of the diocese normally ordains the priests and deacons of his diocese and must authorize all priests who enter the diocese to administer the sacraments. You might say that the bishop is the chief priest in each diocese—the chief representative of Jesus Christ in his royal priesthood. His main concern is to offer to the Father a people who are holy: "As those who lead others to perfection, bishops should be diligent in fostering holiness among their clerics, religious, and laity according to the special vocation of each . . . . [and] to give an example of holiness through charity, humility, and simplicity of life" (no. 15).

Perhaps the most striking and important of all the roles of the bishop presented by Vatican II is how the bishop carries out the kingly ministry of Christ. Far from "lording it over" his flock, the bishop is presented as a "good shepherd" and a "true father" to his people: "In exercising his office of father and pastor, a bishop should stand in the midst of his people as one who serves [cf. Lk 22:26-27]. Let him be a good shepherd who knows his sheep and whose sheep know him. Let him be a true father who excels in a spirit of love and solicitude for all. . . . Let him so gather and mold the whole family of his flock that everyone, conscious of his own duties, may live and work in the communion of love. . . ." (no. 16).

Many other aspects of the bishop's pastoral role are mentioned, such as his ecumenical concern (no. 16), his promotion of the lay apostolate (no. 17), and care for other groups in need (no. 18). But what stands out is the fatherly and fraternal care that the bishop is to have for all people whom he is called to serve, and his responsibility to preach and teach the Catholic faith in its fullness.

How do priests collaborate with their bishops?

The Extraordinary Synod of 1985 speaks of priests having a participation in the bishop's ministry, and thus a co-responsibility with him for the life and leadership of the church. As the Synod states:

> Between a Bishop and his presbyterate there exists a relationship founded on the Sacrament of Orders. Thus priests in a certain way make the Bishop present in the individual local assemblies of the faithful, and assume and exercise in part, in their daily work, his tasks and his solicitude (cf. LG, no. 28). Consequently, friendly relations and full trust must exist between Bishops and their priests.

> Bishops feel themselves linked in gratitude to their priests, who in the post-conciliar period have played a

great part in implementing the Council (cf. **OI**, no. 1), and they wish to be close with all their strength to their priests and to give them help and support in their often difficult work, especially in parishes" (**ES**, pp. 57-58).

The priest shares in the fullness of the ministerial priesthood possessed by the bishop. He participates in a way similar to the bishop in Jesus' roles of priest, prophet, and king. The Second Vatican Council's *Decree on the Ministry and Life of Priests* (**PO**, *Presbyterorum ordinis*), states that priests ". . . have as their primary duty the proclamation of the gospel of God to all . . . not to teach their own wisdom but God's Word, and to summon all men urgently to conversion and holiness" (**PO**, no. 4).

"The source and the apex of the whole work of preaching the gospel . . ." is the Eucharist, over which the priest presides and strives to lead the faithful "to an ever-improved spirit of prayer" (no. 5). Priests extend the praise and thanksgiving of the Eucharist to the different hours of the day by reciting the Divine Office or Liturgy of the Hours.

As pastors or shepherds, the priest reflects the same fatherly care for the faithful as the bishop. Indeed, a priest is called "Father" in the Catholic tradition because he is a "father in Christ Jesus" to his people (see 1 Cor 4:15), and mirrors the love of God the Father to all. The decree notes that "priests must treat all with outstanding humanity, in imitation of the Lord. They should act toward men, not as seeking to win their favor but in accord with the demands of Christian doctrine and life" (no. 6).

There is no room for priests who are after popularity or who promote the values of the world. ". . . priests are never to put themselves at the service of any ideology or human faction. Rather, as heralds of the gospel and shepherds of the Church, they must devote themselves to the spiritual growth of the Body of Christ" (no. 6). The goal of their ministry is to lead people to Christian maturity (no. 6).

As if this were not enough of a challenge, one short section of this decree catalogues those for whom priests are to have a *special* care: the poor and the lowly, youth, married people and parents, all religious men and women, and above all, the sick and the dying (no. 6). The same section proceeds to explain that "the office of pastor is not confined to the care of the faithful as *individuals*, but is also properly extended to the *formation of a genuinely Christian community* ... [which] should not only promote the care of its own faithful, but filled with a missionary zeal, it should also prepare the way to Christ for all men" (no. 6, emphasis mine).

How are priests to fulfill these "superhuman" responsibilities?

It would be tragic and irresponsible if priests were given this tremendous list of duties and responsibilities, without a corresponding list of resources and means of support for their lives and ministries. *The Decree on the Ministry and Life of Priests* includes the following sources of strength for priests.

First, a good relationship with the bishop is key. He "should regard priests as his brothers and friends ... [and] should have at heart the material and especially spiritual welfare of his priests. For above all, upon the bishop rests the heavy responsibility for the sanctity of his priests" (no. 7).

Second, holiness or sanctity is the key to a priest's ability to carry out his ministry successfully, because his relationship with God is the priest's primary support. Chapter 3 discusses the priestly call to perfection, which is fostered especially by daily Eucharist and the daily reading of God's Word in Scripture (no. 13), as well as by the other sacraments, spiritual reading, especially "a study of the Holy Fathers and Doctors and other annals of tradition ..." (no. 19), mortification (no. 12), the Divine Office, and personal prayer.

Third, priests must support and help each other in various

ways. Older priests should help younger priests and vice versa. There should be hospitality and recreation among priests, some form of community life, and associations for mutual support and growth in holiness (no. 18).

Fourth, lay persons may be a significant personal support and source of practical assistance in ministry for priests (no. 9). They must especially pray for their priests (no. 11). Some lay people may even form a deep personal friendship with a priest.

Finally, priests should receive a just recompense for their service, and have a "vacation each year" (no. 20).

It is encouraging to see that the support for priests includes both the spiritual and the human dimensions!

Is it true that a priest does not need to be particularly holy?

All of us, including priests, are sinners who are redeemed and being redeemed by Jesus Christ. The Council reaffirms its long-held teaching that ". . . the grace of God can complete the work of salvation even through unworthy ministers." This is the sacramental doctrine of *ex opere operato;* the efficacy of the sacrament does not depend on the worthiness of the minister. "Yet ordinarily God desires to manifest His wonders through those who have been made particulary docile to the impulse and guidance of the Holy Spirit. Because of their intimate union with Christ and their holiness of life, these men can say with the Apostle: 'It is now no longer I that live, but Christ lives in me' (Gal 2:20)" (**PO**, no. 12). Priests should be holy to reflect the holiness of God.

Isn't celibacy a stumbling block for many priests?

Vatican II responds that even though celibacy is "not demanded by the very nature of the priesthood," it "accords with the priesthood" in many ways. Jesus himself recommended it (Mt 19:12), and priests consecrated to him in this way "more easily hold fast to Him with undivided heart" (**PO**, no. 16).

The "marriage" of the priest to Christ evokes the marriage of the church to Christ that will be fully manifested when Christ returns. At that time, marriage between man and woman will cease (Lk 20:35-36) and only marriage to Christ will remain. Priests become "a vivid sign of that future world which is already present through faith and charity, ..." (no. 16). Hence, priestly celibacy is recommended by the Lord, fosters undivided devotion and service to him, and is a sign of that total union with Christ in the world to come.

The document observes that "many men today call perfect continence impossible" (no. 16). The solution proposed is for priests and the whole church to pray perseveringly for the grace of fidelity which "is never denied to those who ask" (no. 16). Also, priests must "make use of all the supernatural and natural helps" to live this calling, especially by observing the ascetical norms that have been tested by the church's experience. Some of these norms simply regard due care in relating to women and watching over one's eyes and thoughts in order to preserve chastity. Friendships and other healthy, supportive relationships with other priests, and with religious and lay people, can also be helpful to a priest in living out his celibate commitment.

With regard to a decline in vocations, *The Decree on the Ministry and Life of Priests* emphasizes that God is committed to providing priests for his church. It is the duty of the whole Christian people to cooperate with God's will for priestly vocations "by constant prayer and other means at their disposal, so that the Church may always have the necessary number of priests to carry out her divine mission" (no. 2). Recently I heard that vocations to the priesthood in a particular diocese are increasing rapidly since parishes in the diocese started devoting periods of Eucharistic adoration specifically to pray for vocations to the priesthood.

Prayer is a key to priestly vocations.

Other means to foster vocations are discussed at length in chapter 2 of *The Decree on Priestly Formation*. In this task, the whole Christian community, families, parishes, teachers, priests, and bishops all have a role to play. Parents certainly can encourage their boys to consider a priestly vocation and to enable them to get to know priests. Parishes can involve boys and young men in the service of God, such as by training and using altar boys in the liturgy.

The pastor or other priests might get involved in sodalities, youth groups, sports, scouts, CCD, and other youth activities. Single adult men may be encouraged to get involved in leadership roles in the parish or diocese. One of my best friends was teaching as a single layman at a Catholic college. The bishop got to know him and put him on the diocesan priestly vocations' committee. The bishop asked him one day if he might have a vocation to the priesthood! Now my friend is a priest of that diocese, teaching in a prominent Catholic seminary.

At Franciscan University of Steubenville, we have a commitment to encourage priestly and religious vocations. Our goal is that God would be given a "tithe" of 10 percent of our student body entering priesthood or religious life. We have had close to that percentage attained in our recent graduating classes. Our pre-theologate program and household on campus for young men considering a vocation to the priesthood has been a successful channel for God's call to priesthood to be discovered and pursued here.

The approach of Vatican II to priestly vocations does *not* include loosening the requirements for priesthood. In fact, it insists that "necessary standards must always be firmly maintained, even when there exists a regrettable shortage of priests. For God will not allow His Church to lack ministers if worthy candidates are admitted . . ." (**OT**, no. 6). Neither does the Council consider changing the law of celibacy for the Latin rite Catholic church, allowing a married clergy, although this discipline theoretically could be changed. Instead the Council calls the church to faith, prayer, and the living of a vibrant, dedicated Christian life that will attract candidates to the priesthood.

Have we been too ready in the past twenty-five years to consider *other solutions* to the problems of the exodus of priests from active ministry and the decline in priestly vocations? Have we really pursued the solutions recommended by the Council? Do we have enough faith to see the priesthood flourish and triumph even as a small band, like Gideon's army? Just as the small group of apostles and Christians of the primitive church "conquered the world" through their witness, a small but dedicated and holy band of celibate priests can, with God's help, accomplish his will beyond our imagining. It is upon this faith that the Council's teaching rests.

What other special counsels are priests called to embrace?

As we have noted, celibacy is an expression of chastity embraced by priests in the Latin rite or Roman Catholic church, while many priests and ministers in Eastern rite Catholic churches and other Christian bodies follow the gospel's call to chastity through faithfulness and continence in marriage. Religious also voluntarily live chaste celibacy through vows or promises to follow Christ in this way. Celibacy is a sign of special dedication to Christ and a foreshadowing of the world to come where we will neither marry nor be given in marriage. In the sex-saturated culture of the West, the sign of a committed celibate life or a faithful marriage is a powerful witness to the gospel of Christ.

Besides chastity, the Catholic church has always honored in a special way the two other "evangelical (gospel) counsels": poverty and obedience. The vows that characterize religious life are vows to live faithfully the "evangelical counsels" of voluntary poverty, chaste celibacy, and obedience. Priests in religious orders take these three vows. Diocesan priests in Roman Catholicism promise to live a celibate life in obedience to the pope, to their bishop, and to any others in legitimate authority over them in the church. For example, a priest serving as an assistant pastor in a parish is obedient to the pastor. Even though diocesan priests do not take a vow of poverty, "they are invited to embrace voluntary poverty. By it they will be more clearly likened to Christ and will become more devoted to the sacred ministry. For Christ became poor for our sakes, ..." (**PO**, no. 17).

Commitments to voluntary poverty and obedience in imitation of Christ, like that of chaste celibacy, are not easy in a world which often flaunts and praises unrestricted sex, materialism and consumerism, independence, and rebellion against authority. Yet this is what makes the living of these challenging gospel counsels central to the Catholic challenge to the world. Far from being outmoded, the traditional Catholic practice of poverty, chastity, and obedience (by priests, religious, *and* lay people), is a more powerful witness than ever to the presence of Jesus Christ and to the eternal values of his kingdom.

What about the ordination of women to the priesthood?

There is no direct discussion of this issue in *The Decree on the Ministry and Life of Priests* or any other document of the Second Vatican Council. However, the Council defends the rights of women (see **GS**, no. 29) and calls for an increased participation of women in the life and mission of the church (see **AA**, no. 9).

Concerning the ordination of women, the declaration of the Sacred Congregation of the Doctrine of the Faith, *On the Question of the Admission of Women to the Ministerial Priesthood,* (Oct. 15, 1976), and the teaching of recent popes, including Pope John Paul II, affirm and explain the reasons for the unbroken tradition of the Catholic church, now nearly two thousand years old, on this issue. Since these reasons were not debated at Vatican II and are not part of the Council documents, I refer the reader to the above declaration or to my article, "Women Priests," in the January, 1989 issue of *New Covenant* magazine.[1]

As we see from the example of countless women saints, both lay and religious, there has never been a lack of women leading the church to sanctity through their example and teaching. The Extraordinary Synod of 1985 urges the church to "do its utmost so that [women] might be able to express, in the service of the Church, their own gifts, and to play a greater part in the various fields of the Church's apostolate (cf. **AA**, no. 9). May pastors gratefully accept and promote the collaboration of women in ecclesial activity" (**ES**, p. 58).

Did Vatican II introduce any significant changes in priestly formation?

Vatican II's *Decree on Priestly Formation* presents some general rules that need to be applied, and sometimes adapted, by episcopal conferences throughout the world. The document emphasizes the importance of sound theological, spiritual, pastoral, and liturgical formation. It places equal weight on the seminarians' intellectual formation, balanced human development, and emotional maturity (no. 3).

There is no indication that seminarians should be artificially isolated from the world or their families. Their "course of studies ought to be so arranged that students can continue them elsewhere without disadvantage if they choose another state of life" (no. 3). They should be "duly aware of the duties and dignity of Christian marriage, . . . as well [as] the superiority of virginity consecrated to Christ . . ." (no. 10).

What might be most surprising to some is the chapter on ecclesiastical studies (ch. 5). Seminarians are still instructed to "acquire a command of Latin." Philosophy remains at the heart of priestly training, working together harmoniously with theology.

The Extraordinary Synod of 1985 calls attention to article 16 of this decree concerning the manner of teaching theology. First, the Synod teaches that theological studies for seminarians should be based on divine revelation and authentic Catholic doctrine. They should be trained to ". . . understand that doctrine, profoundly nourish their own spiritual lives with it, and be able to proclaim it, unfold it, and defend it in their priestly ministry." Seminarians should be trained with special diligence in sacred Scripture "which ought to be the soul of all theology" (no. 16).

Second, biblical themes are to be presented *first* in dogmatic theology, followed by an historical study of the transmission and development of doctrine through the Catholic tradition.

Third, a strictly Thomistic education is not required, but the meaning of doctrine should be penetrated "more deeply with the help of speculative reason exercised under the tutelage of St. Thomas" (no. 16).

Finally, all other theological studies should flow from the mystery of Christ and the history of salvation, and in moral theology, "its scientific exposition should be more thoroughly nourished by scriptural teaching" (no. 18). The education of seminarians should aim "at a genuine and deep formation of students" (no. 17). Practice in developing the call to the priesthood in pastoral areas is also an indispensable part of this formation. Continuing education of priests is strongly encouraged (no. 22).

The Extraordinary Synod of 1985 particularly highlights the need for formation in holiness. Seminarians need to be formed not only intellectually, but spiritually as well. "They must be seriously introduced to a daily spiritual life: prayer, meditation, the reading of the Bible, the sacraments of Penance and the Eucharist." Also in their pastoral ministry and activity, they need to find spiritual nourishment so that they might truly build up God's people by their example of holiness and offer them correct spiritual counsel and guidance.

Is this a "rosy" picture of the priesthood?

No. The last paragraph of *The Decree on the Ministry and Life of Priests* looks at some of the difficulties which confront priestly life today, including loneliness, social pressures, loss of faith, and "the seeming sterility of their past labors" (no. 22). *The Decree on Priestly Formation* states that in training seminarians ". . . no hardship of priestly life should go unmentioned" including the challenge of celibacy (**OT**, no. 9).

However, amidst the challenges and trials of priestly life, there is an unshakeable source of strength and hope:

Priests should remember that in performing their tasks they are never alone. Relying on the power of Almighty God and believing in Christ Who called them to share in His priesthood, they should devote themselves to their ministry with complete trust, knowing that God can intensify in them the ability to love.

Let them be mindful too that they have as partners their brothers in the priesthood and indeed the faithful of the entire world. For all priests cooperate in carrying out the saving plan of God. (**PO**, no. 22)

With God, their brother priests, and the faithful people of God to support them, priests will find strength and hope even in their most difficult struggles.

What about the renewal of religious life?

The Decree on the Appropriate Renewal of Religious Life (**PC**, ***Perfectae caritatis***) called for these two things to be undertaken simultaneously: First "a continuous *return* to the sources of all Christian life and to the original inspiration behind a given community, and [second] an *adjustment* [or adaptation] of the community to the changed conditions of the times. . . ." (no. 2).

The decree specified that this renewal "should go forward under the influence of the Holy Spirit and the guidance of the Church" according to certain principles. First, the "following of Christ as proposed by the gospel, . . . is to be regarded by all communities as their supreme law," since this is the fundamental norm of religious life.

Second, religious communities each have their own special character and purpose, which is enshrined in "the spirit of [their] founders" and in other traditions at the heart of each community's heritage.

Third, all communities should participate in the life of the church, taking as their own and fostering in every possible way the church's objectives in every field. The mission and goals of the whole church are also to be those of each religious community.

Fourth, members of religious communities must be aware of contemporary human conditions and of the needs of the church, so that they can combine "the burning zeal of an apostle with wise judgments" about the circumstances of the modern world, and hence come to the aid of others more effectively.

Finally, the religious life is intended, above all else, to lead those who embrace it to an imitation of Christ and to union with God through the profession of the evangelical counsels. The fact must be honestly faced that even the most desirable changes made on behalf of contemporary needs will fail unless a renewal of spirit gives life to them. Indeed, such an interior renewal must always be accorded the leading role, even in the promotion of exterior works (**PC**, no. 2).

These principles are to guide the renewal of religious life. Special attention must be given to the last point about the importance of a "renewal of spirit" or interior renewal. The source of this renewal is the gospel of Christ and a discovery or re-discovery of each religious community's foundation and its purpose in the modern world. This conciliar teaching led some Third Order Franciscans to begin studying the origins of their particular branch of the Franciscan family. Although hundreds of small Third Order Franciscan groups exist around the world, they had a very diverse understanding of their particular mission and gift for the church until this historical research was undertaken and meetings of Third Order Franciscan groups from around the world were held. Out of this has come an agreement on the common identity and mission of this branch of the Franciscans, which has led to the updated rewriting of their constitutions, and more significantly a reunification of Franciscan life and spirituality among the Third Order Regular Franciscans and the lay secular Franciscan Order that is associated with it.

It should be noted that there are no directives in the Vatican II decree that justify a compromise of basic gospel values, such as "dying to sin" and "renouncing the world" (no. 5). The living of the evangelical counsels with zeal is highlighted by the decree (nos. 12, 13, 14). Community life should follow the example of the primitive church (no. 15). There is to be a certain streamlining or simplification of religious life to remove unnecessary rules and distinctions between persons (no. 15), and to "avoid every appearance of luxury, of excessive wealth, and accumulation of possessions" (no. 13). Religious habits may be adopted that are more suited to modern circumstances, while remaining, "simple and modest, at once poor and becoming" (no. 17) as a sign of consecrated life.

All of these changes are designed to focus attention upon

the heart of religious life and commitment. They are not concessions to the world or current values. Even when adaptations or adjustments to the needs of the present time are made, the decree states that "the missionary spirit" of religious community should by all means be maintained (no. 20).

Whether applied to contemplative communities (no. 7), clerical or lay institutes devoted to the apostolate (no. 8), monasteries (no. 9), lay religious communities of women or men (no. 10), or secular institutes (no. 11), the focus of *The Decree on the Appropriate Renewal of Religious Life* is on a more fervent and dedicated following of Jesus Christ and his teaching in the modern world.

If this is so, why have so many left the religious life?

Confusion was not *caused* primarily by the Council document. The principles stated there are sound and readily understandable. What happened? Religious communities were challenged to a monumental task: to reexamine every aspect of their identity and lives and to conform these to the standards of the gospel, their founding vision and heritage, and to the new circumstances and needs of the present time. This is a "tall order"!

Obviously some difficulty would result when members of religious communities met to discuss and decide *how* to remain loyal to the spirit of the founder, and *how* to adapt to modern circumstances without compromising essentials. It was a matter of balancing many important values and demands, especially when what was right and wrong was not clear, but a matter of discernment. In the process, many religious whose vocation was not firm, or who had depended unduly on certain external or secondary expressions of religious life, naturally had a difficult time.

Second, there are many forces in the world vying for the allegiance and support of religious communities. In the process of renewal, some communities lost a clear sense of the basic identity and purpose of religious life. Other religious communities may have lost the sense of their own unique calling and mission, instead becoming caught up in other agendas and causes.

Without a firm grasp of the reason for and importance of one's identity and mission in Christ and his church, it is understandable how a religious community having such an identity crisis could struggle, decline, and even disappear.

What is the solution to this crisis in religious life?

Twenty-five years after the Council, we see certain religious communities flourishing and joyfully carrying on the mission of Christ in full loyalty to the teaching of the church. As a result of the renewal of Franciscan life mentioned earlier, I have witnessed the phenomenal growth of orders such as the Third Order Franciscan Sisters of the Sorrowful Mother, which has grown to thirty members in the three years since its inauguration. The church has also witnessed the rapid growth of Mother Teresa's Missionaries of Charity and other religious orders rooted in prayer and loyalty to the church's magisterium.

We see other communities that are holding their ground, but are still very much in the process of discerning their identity and mission. Finally, we observe other communities whose relationship to the official leadership of the Catholic church, to the original mission of their founders, and even to the basic Gospel message, is tenuous or uncertain.

It would seem reasonable to look for guidance and direction for the future to religious communities which are flourishing and have most faithfully responded to the authentic norms of renewal as presented in this Vatican II decree.

Catholics also should look to the example and intercession of Mary, the Mother of God. The decree on religious life closes with these words: "With the prayerful aid of that most loving Virgin Mary, God's Mother, 'whose life is a rule of life for all,' religious communities will experience a daily growth in numbers, and will yield a richer harvest of fruits that bring salvation" (no. 25).

Conclusion

In the last two chapters, we have explored what the Second Vatican Council teaches about the unique gifts and call of the laity, bishops, priests and deacons, and religious. They are called together as members of one people, working together to advance the cause of Jesus Christ and the mission for which he founded the church. Above all, that mission is to bring the good news of salvation in Jesus Christ to all people. The next chapter will explore that great "missionary challenge" to the people of God: to make disciples of all nations (Mt 28:19).

RECOMMENDED READING

*Decree on the Bishops' Pastoral Office in the Church (**Christus Dominus**)*, Abbott ed., pp. 396-429; Flannery ed., pp. 564-590.

*Decree on the Ministry and Life of Priests (**Presbyterorum ordinis**)*, Abbott ed., pp. 532-576; Flannery ed., pp. 863-902.

*Decree on Priestly Formation (**Optatum totius**)*, Abbott ed., pp. 437-457; Flannery ed., pp. 707-724.

QUESTIONS FOR GROUP DISCUSSION

1. Why did Vatican II emphasize the concept of the "collegiality" of the bishops? What are some practical

consequences and expressions of that collegiality since Vatican II?

2. What is an episcopal conference? A Synod of Bishops? How do these express the collegiality of the bishops?

3. How did the Second Vatican Council speak of the pastoral or shepherding role of bishops and priests? What are the implications of this teaching?

4. How can priests be better supported and prepared for their challenging ministry today? What are the positive values which the Roman Catholic church sees in priestly celibacy? Discuss.

5. What is the unique witness of religious in the world today through embracing vows of poverty, chaste celibacy, and religious obedience? What "good fruit" has been brought forth through the renewal of religious life, according to the norms of the decree on the religious life? What are the challenges and problems? Discuss.

PERSONAL CHALLENGE

If you are a bishop, priest, or religious, you are well aware of the daily challenges confronting you and those you serve. But are you familiar with the gospel challenge and hope presented by the Second Vatican Council? All Catholics would benefit from becoming more aware of the guidelines for the renewal of the ministry and life of bishops, priests, and religious that are found in these decrees.

If you are a lay person, ask yourself: Do I understand the purpose and nature of these vocations and ministries in the church, as set forth by Vatican II? How can I better support bishops, priests, and religious in their service of God and his people? Am I seeking God daily for strength, wisdom, and support in the renewal of my own vocation and ministry in the church, so that I can support and strengthen others? Do I forget that those dedicated to God's service as bishops, priests or religious are human beings who need encouragement, affirmation, and prayer? How can I provide these, even in a small way? Do I at least pray for the sisters, brothers, priests, deacons, and the bishop who serve me?

RESOURCE LIST

Through the Priestly Ministry, the Gift of Salvation: Messages of John Paul II to Bishops, Priests, and Deacons, Vols. 1 and 2, (Boston, MA: Daughters of St. Paul, 1982).

Essential Elements in the Church's Teaching on Religious Life, Pope John Paul II, May 31, 1983.

EIGHT

Proclaiming the Gospel

THIS CHAPTER WILL DISCUSS three documents of the Second Vatican Council that are closely related: *The Declaration on Religious Freedom* (**DH**, *Dignitatis humanae*), *The Declaration on the Relationship of the Church to Non-Christian Religions* (**NA**, *Nostra aetate*), and *The Decree on the Missionary Activity of the Church* (**AG**, *Ad gentes*). What these documents have in common is that they all describe basic attitudes that Catholics must have as they approach non-Christians. We must defend the freedom of others to believe what they want and to practice their religion freely. We must respect whatever is true and good in other religions. And we must tirelessly witness in word and deed to the *fullness* of truth revealed in Jesus Christ to those who do not yet know or believe in him.

There are many misconceptions about the teaching of Vatican II on these topics. Some Catholics, even missionaries, are not aware that the Council clearly teaches that the gospel of Christ must be proclaimed. This is an urgent command from the Lord that is central to the church's mission. Although missionaries should also seek to alleviate hunger and promote the human development of those people to whom they are sent, their *primary mission* is to lead others to faith and life in Christ, and to his church, through which they will find spiritual nourishment and eternal life.

A second common misconception is that the Second Vatican Council encouraged Catholics to seek wisdom and truth from non-Christian religions, even to incorporate certain non-Christian practices into their lives as Christians. This is not the case. It is true that in missionary countries some non-Christian beliefs and practices that are compatible with Christianity may be incorporated into the church's faith and life in some way.

However, this is far different, for example, than Western Christians who seek to incorporate non-Christian elements from other cultures into their own religious practice and belief—as if the rich spiritual tradition of Western Christianity were inadequate or incomplete. Why would a person who owned the world's richest gold mine need to go to the ends of the earth to obtain a few gold pieces from other mines? The owner of the mine might examine them out of curiosity or for comparison, but certainly it would not be necessary to possess them. Catholics of the West should thoroughly mine the rich storehouse of saints and mystics of their own tradition before seeking nuggets of truth elsewhere.

Finally, lest Catholics fall into arrogance or pride, the Second Vatican Council stresses that each Catholic—even bishops and priests—need to be converted ever more deeply to the Lord so that we can be more effective witnesses to Jesus Christ in word and deed. The missionary activity of the church is never completed. It requires our constant transformation by the grace of Christ.

Hence, the challenge presented here by the Second Vatican Council can be simply stated: How do we fulfill Jesus' great commission to his followers, "Go, therefore, and make disciples of all nations . . ." (Mt 28:19)? In the modern context, we recognize that this is part of a broader question that is often asked today: How do Christians view and relate to those who are not Christian? Many specific questions flow from this one: Are they saved? Should Christians work with non-Christians on common projects? Should we dialogue with them or simply try to convert them? Do non-Christians have anything to teach Christians? Could we adopt or adapt some of their religious practices? How should Christianity be adapted to other cultures? If non-Christian religious are *not* true, should they have a right to exist, or do they have any rights?

Let us turn to the Council documents themselves for a response to these issues.

What is the approach of *The Declaration on Religious Freedom?*

The Declaration on Religious Freedom is formally addressed to all people. Sometimes called the American contribution to the Council, it embodies the ideal of religious freedom enunciated by the United States Constitution, including the very phrase concerning the "free exercise of religion" that is found in the First Amendment (no. 1).

However, the concern for religious rights and freedom has been constant in the church for centuries. This declaration openly proclaims its intention "to develop the doctrine of recent Popes on the inviolable rights of the human person and on the constitutional order of society" (no. 1).

This document may be seen as the crown of a long history of the church's deepening insight into this subject, guided by the Holy Spirit. Since the Council, religious freedom has become a hallmark of the teaching of Pope John Paul II in his speeches and pastoral visits.

Although this chapter focuses on the implications of this declaration for the relationship of Catholics to non-Christians, it has monumental significance for the cause of all people who are struggling to secure their religious freedom. Until recently, this struggle was often seen as happening primarily in countries that were openly atheistic or anti-religious, but in an ironic twist, many of those countries are now opening up to religious freedom, while in democratic and traditionally "free" countries like the United States, the free exercise of religion is being threatened and challenged in the courts and legislative bodies.

What is the basis of the Council's teaching on religious freedom?

The Declaration on Religious Freedom is addressed to all people, because it wishes to propound principles that deserve universal recognition. The two basic principles that underlie this concept are: 1.) the dignity of the human person, which dictates that each person be able to exercise responsible freedom and act on his or her own judgment, especially in matters of conscience such as religion; and 2.) the duty of government and society to protect and foster individual rights and freedoms.

The document's argument develops in this way: a) All people are bound to seek the truth and to embrace the truth they come to know. b) The truth must enter a person because he or she is convinced of it. c) Therefore, the acceptance of the truths of religion must be made freely, without any coercion, whether physical or psychological. "Nor is anyone to be restrained from acting in accordance with his own beliefs, whether privately or publicly, whether alone or in association with others, within due limits" (no. 2). d) Because the right to religious freedom is known both through reason and God's revelation, this freedom is to be recognized by governments and societies as an inalienable civil right (no. 2).

How does religious freedom affect our approach to non-Christians?

Lest there be any confusion about what the Catholic church believes, the first paragraph of *The Declaration on*

Religious Freedom announces: "We believe that this one true religion subsists in the Catholic and apostolic Church, to which the Lord Jesus committed the duty of spreading it abroad among all men" (no. 1). Catholics firmly believe that the Christian faith, as taught in fullness by the Catholic church, is the one true religion which God desires all people to embrace.

Nonetheless, this true religion must be embraced in authentic *freedom*. Non-Christians have a right to follow and act according to their beliefs and consciences, especially in religious matters. Even in predominantly Catholic countries in which Catholicism is established by law as the "official" religion, it is essential that the right of all citizens and religious bodies to religious freedom be recognized and practically respected (no. 6).

Likewise, in countries in which the Catholic faith is not officially recognized or established, such as in non-Christian nations, the Catholic church claims freedom for herself and for all others. Individuals and groups should be able to practice and profess their faith freely and openly, in private and in public, without restraint or coercion, as long as the rights of others and the genuine common good are respected and upheld (no. 13).

Catholics reject all forms of coercion or undue pressure in bringing non-Christians to the Catholic faith. This would include promises of political or economic advantage, food or other gifts, that would be offered to a person for becoming a Catholic. The document teaches that "in spreading religious faith and in introducing religious practices, everyone ought at all times to refrain from any manner of action which might seem to carry a hint of coercion or of a kind of persuasion that would be dishonorable or unworthy, especially when dealing with poor or uneducated people" (no. 4; see also **AG**, no. 13). The Catholic church openly admits in the same document that its members have sometimes violated this teaching, although the church has always firmly taught it (no. 12).

How does Jesus exemplify this teaching?

Both Jesus and the early church acknowledged the rights of civil government. Yet the early church "did not hesitate to speak out against governing powers which set themselves in opposition to the holy will of God: 'We must obey God rather than man' (Acts 5:29)."

Both Jesus and the early church boldly proclaimed the truth without imposing it by force on anyone. "They preached the Word of God in the full confidence that there was resident in this Word itself a divine power able to destroy all the forces arrayed against God and to bring man to faith in Christ and to His service" (**DH**, no. 11).

What about the relationship of the church to non-Christian religions?

The declaration on non-Christian religions states that the Council "gives primary consideration in this document to what human beings have in common and to what promotes fellowship among them" (**NA**, no. 1). Realizing that in this age, people of different faiths are being drawn closer together, the Catholic church wishes to present here the basis for respect, cooperation, and fellowship among them.

Catholics are instructed to recognize and respect what is true and holy in non-Christian religions (no. 2), and to root out all discrimination against them because of their beliefs. This latter point is based on Scripture's teaching that we cannot claim to love God, whom we do not see, if we fail to love our brother or sister whom we do see (1 Jn 4:20). All people are created by God in his own image, and Christians must therefore act in a brotherly way towards all.

How do we regard what is "true and holy" in non-Christian religions?

The declaration notes some particular points of agreement between the Catholic faith and Hinduism, Buddhism (no. 2), and Islam (no. 3). These religions "often reflect a ray of that Truth which enlightens all men" (no. 2). The church exhorts Catholics to "prudently and lovingly . . . acknowledge, preserve, and promote the spiritual and moral goods" (no. 2) found among these people.

Fully one-third of the declaration is devoted to the relationship of Catholics to the Jewish people, who share with Christians a close spiritual bond. The Catholic church recognizes that "the Jews still remain most dear to God because of their fathers" (no. 4), and wishes to foster with the Jewish people ". . . that mutual understanding and respect which is the fruit above all of biblical and theological studies, and of brotherly dialogue" (no. 4).

It is clear from this that neither the Jewish people nor other non-Christians possess the fullness of truth in Christ that resides in the Catholic church. Nor is there any indication in this document that Catholics should adopt or integrate into their own beliefs or practices any of those found in non-Christian religions. We are to acknowledge and affirm in them whatever "ray" or portion of the truth which they happen to possess.

It is disconcerting to observe that Catholics today often seek spiritual truth and religious practices in non-Christian religions, while failing to explore and integrate all the rich treasures found in the two-thousand-year-old spiritual tradition of Catholic Christianity. There is a big difference between respecting truths and goodness found in non-Christian religions (which the Council approves), and the syncretism of adopting these beliefs as part of Catholic life, worship, or theology, which the Council does not call for.

What about religious persecution and discrimination?

The declaration calls for an end to all quarrels and ". . . any discrimination against men or harassment of them because of their race, color, condition of life, or religion" (no. 5). It calls for Christians and Moslems ". . . to forget the past and to strive sincerely for mutual understanding" (no. 3).

A serious statement of reconciliation is made regarding the Jewish people. Article 4 states, first, that the death of Jesus ". . . cannot be blamed upon all the Jews then living, without distinction, nor upon the Jews of today." Second, the Catholic church "repudiates all persecutions," and "deplores the hatred, persecutions, and displays of anti-Semitism directed against the Jews at any time or from any source."[1]

Third, the Catholic church proclaims that Christ "freely underwent His passion and death because of the sins of all men, so that all might attain salvation. It is, therefore, the duty of the Church's preaching to proclaim the cross of Christ as the sign of God's all-embracing love and as the fountain from which every grace flows. . . ." (no. 4).

Rather than discrimination or persecution, the Second Vatican Council points to the sacrificial death of Christ as the sign of God's unconditional love for all people. Christians are to reflect this love and compassion in their attitudes and dealings with all.

Can non-Christians be saved?

Yes, non-Christians *can* be saved, but not all *will* be saved. That non-Christians can be saved is affirmed by this declaration: "His saving designs extend to all men (cf. Wis 8:1; Acts 14:17; Rom 2:6-7; 1 Tm 2:4)" (**NA**, no. 1), and by *The Dogmatic Constitution on the Church,* no. 16, which states:

> Those also can attain to everlasting salvation who through no fault of their own do not know the gospel of Christ or His Church, yet sincerely seek God and, moved by grace, strive by their deeds to do His will as it is known to them through the dictates of conscience. Nor does divine Providence deny the help necessary for salvation to those who, without blame on their part, have not yet

arrived at an explicit knowledge of God, but who strive to live a good life, thanks to His grace. (**LG**, no. 16)

We conclude that non-Christians *can* be saved who meet a number of important conditions: 1.) through no fault of their own they do not *know* the gospel of Christ (and thus have not rejected the truth), 2.) they sincerely seek God, 3.) they strive by God's grace to live a good life and do God's will as they know it through the dictates of conscience.

Do non-Christians then need to hear the gospel of Jesus Christ?

We have just summarized the Council's teaching indicating that it is *possible* for non-Christians to be saved, by the sheer mercy of God. However, as *The Dogmatic Constitution on the Church* proceeds to explain, the goodness and truth that may be found in non-Christian religions are only partial and dim reflections of the fullness of life, grace, and truth that reside in the gospel of Jesus Christ. The constitution states: "Whatever goodness or truth is found among [non-Christians] is looked upon by the Church as a preparation for the gospel. She regards such qualities as given by Him who enlightens all men so that they may finally have life" (no. 16; see also **AG**, no. 2).

In sum, the "rays" of the truth and goodness found in non-Christian religions are intended by God to lead their members to the source and fullness of the truth found in the Son, the Son of God made man, Jesus Christ. Possessing partial truth and goodness does *not* always and necessarily lead to full truth and goodness, nor to eternal salvation. The constitution boldly states: "But rather often men, deceived by the Evil One, have become caught up in futile reasoning and have exchanged the truth of God for a lie, serving the creature rather than the Creator (cf. Rom 1:21, 25). Or some there are who, living and dying in a world without God, are subject to utter hopelessness" (**LG**, no. 16).

The constitution acknowledges the reality that the kingdom of God is engaged in a cosmic battle against the Evil One, Satan, and that there are many casualties. Satan is striving to lead people away from the truth and goodness. "Rather often" (not rarely or even half the time), he succeeds. The problem with possessing only part of the truth of Christ and a portion of his grace, is that it is easier for such a person to end up denying God, serving false gods (including money, power, sex, etc.), or falling into despair, and thus possibly fail to attain eternal life.

What are Christians to do about this? The very next sentence which concludes and completes this section regarding non-Christian religions, gives us the answer: "Consequently, to promote the glory of God and procure the salvation of all such men, and mindful of the command of the Lord, 'Preach the gospel to every creature' (Mk 16:16), the Church painstakingly fosters her missionary work" (**LG**, no. 16).

Now we understand the reason behind the missionary challenge to Catholics. Without the proclamation of the gospel of Jesus Christ, "rather often" those who do not know Christ will fail to attain salvation. Even more importantly, Jesus himself commanded his followers to preach the gospel to every creature and to make disciples of all nations (Mt 28:19). God's will is that all come to salvation through believing the good news of Jesus Christ. The Council declares: "This missionary activity finds its reason in the will of God, 'who wishes all men to be saved and to come to the knowledge of the truth. For there is one God, and one Mediator between God and men, himself man, Christ Jesus, who gave himself a ransom for all' (1 Tm 2:4-5). 'Neither is there salvation in any other' (Acts 4:12)" (**AG**, no. 7).

If this were not yet clear enough, the next section of *The Dogmatic Constitution on the Church* (no. 17) is dedicated entirely to the church's missionary outreach. The Holy

Spirit compels the church to proclaim the gospel since God has established Christ as "the source of salvation for the whole world." The same Spirit prepares those who hear the gospel to believe it and be baptized, so that they are snatched from "the slavery of error" and invited to grow up into full maturity in Christ.

The Council even boldly states that whatever good is found in non-Christian religions . . . "is not only saved from destruction" by acceptance of the gospel of Christ, . . . "but is also healed, ennobled, and perfected unto the glory of God, the confusion of the devil, and the happiness of man." This missionary work is so essential to the life and mission of the church that every disciple of Christ is obligated to participate in it according to his or her ability (**LG**, no. 17; see also **AG**, no. 9).

Isn't there a conflict between the call to dialogue and the call to conversion?

No. Concerning dialogue with non-Christians, the Extraordinary Synod of 1985 stated: "Dialogue must not be opposed to mission. Authentic dialogue tends to bring the human person to open up and communicate his interiority to the one with whom he is speaking. Moreover, all Christians have received from Christ the mission to make all people disciples of Christ (Mt 28:18). In this sense God can use the dialogue between Christians and non-Christians and between Christians and non-believers as a pathway for communicating the fullness of grace" (**ES**, p. 65).

When Christians open themselves to communicate what is most important to them with non-Christians in authentic dialogue, they will witness to the gospel of Jesus Christ, as well as listening to the important values and beliefs of the partner in the dialogue. In this way, the dialogue may become as Pope John Paul II has called it, a "dialogue of salvation." The work of Catholic missionaries, then, may include or even begin with "dialogue," but this must always lead to a clear call to faith in God through Jesus Christ, through whom we receive life and salvation.

What is the missionary task of the church and how does it differ from "evangelization"?

The Decree on the Missionary Activity of the Church (**AG**, *Ad gentes divinitus*) explains that "the pilgrim Church is missionary by her very nature. For it is from the mission of the Son and the mission of the Holy Spirit that she takes her origin, in accordance with the decree of God the Father" (no. 2).

The church itself is the result of God's own missionary activity! Jesus was sent on mission by the Father to establish God's kingdom on earth (no. 3). The Father and the Son sent the Holy Spirit on mission to give birth to the church at Pentecost (no. 4). The church continues the mission of spreading the message and the reality of the kingdom of God " . . . in obedience to Christ's command and in response to the grace and love of the Holy Spirit" (no. 5).

The general term for spreading the gospel and converting others to Jesus Christ is "evangelization." Pope Paul VI's great apostolic exhortation, *On Evangelization in the Modern World* (Dec. 8, 1975) explains that the church "exists in order to evangelize, that is to say in order to preach and teach, to be the channel of the gift of grace, to reconcile sinners with God" (no. 14).

The Extraordinary Synod notes that, "evangelization takes place through witnesses. The witness gives his testimony not only with words, but also with his life." It is not coincidental that the Greek word for testimony is *martyrium*. The ultimate witness is the martyr, who testifies by losing his life for the faith.

What, then, distinguishes missionary activity from evangelization? The term "missions" usually refers to: "preaching the gospel and planting the Church among peoples or groups who do not yet believe in Christ. . . . The specific *purpose* of this missionary activity is evangelization and the planting of the Church among those peoples and groups where she has not yet taken root. . . . The chief *means* of this implantation is the preaching of the gospel of Jesus Christ" (**AG**, no. 6).

Is missionary activity really all that urgent?

In 1965, the Second Vatican Council reported that "the gospel message has not yet been heard, or scarcely so, by two billion human beings. And their number is increasing daily. . . ." (**AG**, no. 10). Even if more people have heard of Jesus Christ, millions do not yet believe in him. Statistics from 1989 estimate that the world population is now composed of about 19 percent Catholics, 14 percent other Christians, and 67 percent non-Christians. Two-thirds of the world's people do not believe in Jesus Christ! The urgency of missionary activity is evident.

The Decree on the Church's Missionary Activity, article 7, sets forth a bold and impassioned challenge to the church to engage in missionary activity. The document concludes:

Therefore, *all* must be converted to Him as He is made known in the Church's preaching. *All* must be incorporated to Him by baptism, and into the Church which is His body. . . . though God in ways known only to Himself can lead those inculpably ignorant of the gospel to that faith without which it is impossible to please Him (Heb 11:6), yet a necessity lies upon the Church (cf. 1 Cor 9:16), and at the same time a sacred duty, to preach the gospel. Hence missionary activity today as always retains its power and necessity. (no. 7)

Why do many Catholics lack a zeal to evangelize or to do missionary work?

"Why did twelve fishermen convert the world, and why are half a billion Christians unable to repeat the feat? The Spirit makes the difference."[2]

That the Holy Spirit is the source of zeal and power for evangelization and mission is evident from the Acts of the Apostles and Jesus' own teaching. This is why Pope John XXIII accompanied the convocation of Vatican II with prayer for a "new Pentecost," in which the Lord would "renew his wonders in our time."

Many signs indicate that the Catholic church has experienced some of the grace of Pentecost since the close of the Council. Nonetheless, in his recent (Dec. 1988) apostolic letter on the laity, Pope John Paul II called for a *re-evangelization* of Christian countries, whose "moral and spiritual patrimony ... [is under attack from] secularization and a spread of sects. Only a re-evangelization can answer the growth of a clear and deep faith" (**CL**, no. 34).

Obviously, countries which are losing or weakening in the Catholic faith themselves will not readily be in a position to evangelize or send missionaries to others. The same is true on a personal level. If we lack the zeal to evangelize others, either we are not fully converted or empowered to witness ourselves, or else we lack an understanding of the church's missionary nature. The Extraordinary Synod of 1985 states bluntly: "The evangelization of non-believers in fact presupposes the self-evangelization of the baptized and also, in a certain sense, of deacons, priests, and Bishops" (**ES**, p. 50).

How remarkable that a group of bishops would openly acknowledge that even they, the bishops, need to evangelize themselves! And yet only this sort of humility will enable Catholics to turn to God in prayer and repentance. We need to ask him for the same boldness and power of the

Holy Spirit that first filled the apostles and the early church at Pentecost. Only this will enable Catholics to evangelize others, and to support the missionaries called by God to plant the gospel where it has never been heard.

I frequently hear from people about non-denominational or Pentecostal churches that are made up largely of ex-Catholics. Apparently many Catholics think that they have not heard the basic gospel message clearly proclaimed in the Catholic church and have gone elsewhere. This is why our own church needs to be re-evangelized, so it is clear to all that the Catholic church is rooted and constantly nourished in the *full gospel* of Christ.

The saying, "You can't give what you ain't got" is also an important truth. Only after this re-evangelization can Catholics undertake what Pope John Paul II set forth as "a giant step forward" in his challenge to the laity: a renewed effort in the evangelization of the world. "The Church today ought to take *a giant step forward* in her evangelization effort, and enter into *a new stage of history* in her missionary dynamism. In a world where the lessening of distance makes the world increasingly smaller, the Church community ought to strengthen the bonds among its members, exchange vital energies and means, and commit itself as a group to a unique and common mission of proclaiming and living the Gospel . . ." (**CL**, no. 35).

Does missionary activity include social justice and service to the poor?

Yes. Missionary activity includes care for persons in every aspect of their lives, including physical needs and human rights and freedoms. A complete view of missionary activity contains many elements. We see this in chapter 2 of *The Decree on Missionary Activity* which divides "mission work itself" into three parts.

The first part discussed is "Christian witness"—the

witness to Christ by both word and deed. This section recommends drawing people to Christ "through truly human conversations" and insists on the importance of knowing the people, their culture, social life, and national and religious traditions (no. 11).

Christian charity extended toward all is at the heart of this witness. The examples offered demonstrate that there is no human struggle or concern outside of the scope of the church's missionary endeavor. Rather than contribute mere material progress and prosperity, the ultimate goal of the missionary is "to render to others true witness of Christ, and to work for their salvation" (no. 12).

The second part focuses on the church's missionary task of *preaching the gospel.* Christians should take advantage of any open door and announce "to all men with confidence and constancy the living God, and He whom He has sent for the salvation of all, Jesus Christ" (no. 13). The section notes that initial conversion to Christ must be completed by an ever-deeper ongoing conversion (no. 13).

The third part deals with *forming the Christian community.* Missionaries are urged to "raise up congregations of the faithful" as a sign of God's presence in the world and a means to forming those who have been converted to Christ (no. 15).

To sum up, "it is not enough for the Christian people to be present and organized in a given nation. Nor is it enough for them to carry out an apostolate of good example. They are organized and present for the purpose of announcing Christ to their non-Christian fellow citizens by word and deed, and of aiding them toward the full reception of Christ" (no. 15).

Who carries out the missionary work of the church?

Many are involved, and a variety of ministries are necessary. The bishops who oversee and direct missionary work must have a missionary vision and zeal. Priests and deacons are needed, and "new churches" are encouraged to form their own indigenous clergy. Men and women catechists are of "maximum importance," especially due to the shortage of priests (no. 17). Religious orders are important, too. Finally, the laity "have the greatest importance," especially as they bring the gospel into the everyday life of secular society (no. 15).

What is the goal of missionary work?

The final goal of this work is not simply the conversion of individuals, but the planting of new churches. *The Decree on Missionary Activity* explains that the missionary work of the church has been fulfilled when the local church that has been planted "enjoys a certain stability and firmness." This is achieved when the local church has its own supply of priest, religious, and lay people sufficient to keep the church running strong (**AG**, no. 19). Further, the Council urges that the young churches "participate as soon as possible in the universal missionary work of the Church," and send their own missionaries all over the world (no. 20). In fact, the Council Fathers state that one sign of a church reaching maturity is its ability and desire to spread the gospel to others. The goal of the church's missionary activity is to produce new local churches that send missionaries to others! Thus the church grows and more are brought to Christ.

How is Christian faith to be adapted to different cultures?

The question of how Christianity and the life of the church is expressed in different cultures, now commonly called "inculturation," is a question that is as old as the church, and one that has not been finally resolved.

The decree on missionary activity calls for missionaries to

be fully trained in the culture and language of the country to which they are sent (no. 26). The question is dealt with most specifically in article 22 of *The Decree on the Church's Missionary Activity*. It states that the "young Churches" can borrow from their cultures "all those things which can contribute to the glory of their Creator, the revelation of the Savior's grace, or the proper arrangement of Christian life."

But this can only be achieved through theological investigation of sacred Scripture and Tradition in order to see what legitimate adaptations of beliefs and practices of different cultures may be made. Examples of legitimate adaptation would be the use in the liturgy of musical instruments and garb commonly used in the culture, even the use of some new analogies from their own systems of thought to express or explain Christian doctrine. Inappropriate adaptation would be acceptance of thought or practices intrinsically opposed to or incompatible with Christian revelation, such as cannibalism or polygamy.

"Thanks to such a procedure," [of discernment] the decree states, "every appearance of syncretism and of false particularism can be excluded, and Christian life can be accommodated to the genius and the dispositions of each culture. . . . Particular traditions . . . can be illumined by the light of the gospel, and then be taken into Catholic unity" (no. 22). The key is that all customs, traditions, and values of non-Christian origin must be tested and examined in light of the gospel of Jesus Christ.

The Extraordinary Synod of Bishops explains that the Catholic church "takes from every culture all that it encounters of positive value." However, inculturation is not merely an external adaptation of different cultures to Christianity, "because it means the intimate transformation of authentic cultural values" through their immersion in Christ and his gospel.

Sometimes it is thought that when Christianity or Catholicism confronts a new culture, the faith will lose something in the process of adaptation. To the contrary, the church is enriched and the culture is transformed through encounter with the gospel of Jesus Christ.

Conclusion

The Catholic church has two patron saints of the missions, St. Francis Xavier, the great Jesuit missionary, and St. Thérèse of Lisieux, the contemplative Carmelite nun. This shows that everyone has a part to play in the church's missionary activity, whether it be working in the missions, or praying for the missions and the conversion of all people to Christ.

For this to happen, the Second Vatican Council recognizes the need for both conviction about the church's evangelistic and missionary nature, and for the interior conversion and spiritual power necessary to carry out the missionary task. This is the Lord's missionary challenge to the church. The challenge is summarized by *The Decree on the Missionary Activity of the Church,* which reminds us that the whole church is missionary. Evangelization is a duty for *every* Christian. The first thing a Catholic can do to fulfill this obligation to spread the faith is to lead a profoundly Christian life, "for their fervor in the service of God and their charity toward others will cause new spiritual inspiration to sweep over the whole church." The decree adds that ". . . This living testimony will more easily achieve its effect if it is given in unison with other Christian communities, according to the norms of *The Decree on Ecumenism* (nos. 35, 36).

The last thought indicates another challenge to Catholics today. The modern ecumenical movement was born on the mission field, when Protestant missionaries at the turn of the twentieth century realized the scandal that their division caused to non-believers. This motivated them to seek greater unity with each other to promote the gospel of Jesus Christ.

The Second Vatican Council recognizes this same fact. It teaches that although missionary activity differs from ecumenical efforts, these are closely connected. Since the division among Christians obstructs the spread of the gospel, the work of restoring Christian unity also enhances the power of the church's witness of Christ to the world (**AG**, no. 6). The missionary challenge mandates the challenge of ecumenism, which will be the topic of the next chapter.

RECOMMENDED READING

Declaration on Religious Freedom (**Dignitatis humanae**), Abbott ed., pp. 675-696; Flannery ed., pp. 799-812.

Declaration on the Relationship of the Church to Non-Christian Religions (**Nostra aetate**), Abbott ed., pp. 660-668; Flannery ed., pp. 738-742.

Decree on the Missionary Activity of the Church, (**Ad gentes divinitas**), Abbott ed., pp. 584-630; Flannery ed., pp. 813-862.

QUESTIONS FOR GROUP DISCUSSION

1. What is the Catholic church's understanding of "religious freedom"?' What specific freedoms and responsibilities does the "Declaration on Religious Freedom" present and defend?

2. Is there any other savior for humanity than Jesus Christ? How does the Second Vatican Council describe our relationship with and approach to the Jewish people? To other non-Christian religions?

3. What is the difference between "evangelization" and "missionary activity"? Why are both evangelization and missionary activity essential to the church and necessary endeavors for every Catholic?

4. What are some ways that Catholics can evangelize others to Christ and support the church's missionary endeavors? What support, training, or preparation do you think is necessary for you to evangelize or engage in missionary activity effectively? Discuss.

5. Why do many Catholics think that converting non-Christians to Christ and his church is unnecessary, or even secondary to providing for their material needs? Discuss.

PERSONAL CHALLENGE

The Catholic church challenges its members: to *defend* the right of each person to believe what they want about God and to practice their religion freely; to *respect* whatever is true, good, and holy in other religions; to seek to understand the beliefs of others through dialogue; to *witness* boldly to Jesus Christ as the only Savior of the world; and to lead people to the fullness of Christian life, belief, and worship within the Catholic church.

Perhaps the first challenge is to understand these callings as *complementary* and not contradicting each other. The unifying factor of these challenges is to recognize that God made each person to seek him and to worship him in freedom, trusting that all truth ultimately leads to him who is *the* Truth, Jesus Christ. Catholics, along with all Christians, are called by Christ to make disciples of all nations by testifying to the love and mercy of God which shines out in

Jesus' life, death, and resurrection. Through our testimony, the Holy Spirit himself will lead others to the fullness of truth and life found in Jesus alone, manifested most fully in the Catholic church.

Ask yourself: Do I uphold the freedom of others to practice their religion openly, even when their beliefs are contrary to my own? Do I understand that the beliefs of other religions do contain some true and beautiful elements, which may be points of contact in a religious dialogue, perhaps even leading those of other religions to consider the truth and beauty of Christianity? Do I witness to my own faith in Christ with love, sensitivity, and boldness? Do my words as well as my actions testify to Christ? Do I pray for the conversion (or deeper conversion) of others to Christ? Do I take as a personal invitation the call of Jesus Christ and the church for *all* to be witnesses to Christ? Whom do I know now that I could pray for to receive the good news? How might I be a better witness to them of God's love? How might I better prepare myself or find encouragement to share the gospel with others?

RESOURCE LIST

On Evangelization in the Modern World (Evangelii Nuntiandi), Pope Paul VI, December 8, 1975. (Available through the Daughters of St. Paul, Boston, MA, or the Publication Office of the United States Catholic Conference, 1976).

John Paul II: Essays on Religious Freedom, John Paul II (Milwaukee, WI: Catholic League for Religions and Civil Rights, 1984).

NINE

The Call to Christian Unity

T HE PHRASE "To be Catholic is to be ecumenical" best sums up the teaching of the Second Vatican Council on the subject of Christian unity. Pope John XXIII made this a top priority for the Council, and his own efforts in this regard were strikingly successful. Witness, for example, the way he is affectionately remembered, by Catholic and Protestant alike, as "Good Pope John." Now all Catholics have been commissioned by Christ and the church to carry on and advance this mission of Christian unity that is so close to the heart of God himself.

I personally did not become aware of the ecumenical dimension of my faith until I was exposed to the charismatic renewal movement. Through this movement, God brought many Christians of different churches together to pray, to share Scripture, and to love each other in Jesus Christ. The Holy Spirit, who is the source of all true unity, was evidently calling forth Catholics to this new advance in Christian unity that was spoken about theologically by the Second Vatican Council.

The Holy Spirit has continued to foster this work of Christian unity through the emergence of ecumenical groups of committed Christians, such as the "Allies for Faith and Renewal," an annual ecumenical conference coordinated by the Alliance for Faith & Renewal in Ann Arbor, Michigan. From the Catholic charismatic renewal, ecumenical covenant communities have sprung up, such as the one which has helped our small Catholic community in Steubenville, Ohio, to gain a greater ecumenical and missionary perspective. These groups have demonstrated to me that it *is* possible for Christians of different churches to commit themselves to love and serve each other, to pray together, to reach out to the world to bring others to Jesus Christ, and to work together for the transformation of society to Christian values. I have seen all of this occur while members remain loyal and committed to the churches to which they belong.

While not always easy, there are great rewards in following the Lord's call to join together with other Christians in this ecumenical age. More and more we see Christians of different traditions working together side by side in service to the poor, in pro-life activities, and in other outreaches designed to foster the advance of the kingdom of God. Yet Catholics need accurate guidance on proper approaches to dealing and working with other Christians, which we find provided in Vatican II's *Decree on Ecumenism*.

Thus the Second Vatican Council inaugurated a new era in the relationship of Catholics to other Christians. The schism between the Catholic church and the Orthodox churches of the East in 1054 and the Protestant Reformation of the sixteenth century not only divided the one church of Christ, but led to a polarization among Christian bodies. The resulting division was marked by a breakdown in communication, misunderstanding, intolerance, even hostility and open warfare. As Vatican II's *Decree on Ecumenism* (**UR**) observes in its introduction, "Without doubt, this discord openly contradicts the will of Christ, provides a stumbling block to the world, and inflicts damage on the most holy cause of proclaiming the good news to every creature" (no. 1).

Until the twentieth century, Catholics normally felt those who left the Catholic church were responsible for these divisions. The Catholic approach was to pray and work for their return to the "one, true church of Christ"—the Catholic church. Often very little effort was made by Catholics to understand what these other Christians believed. Certainly Catholics seldom appreciated the truly Christian aspects of their beliefs and heritage.

Although the love of Christians for each other had grown cold, "nevertheless, the Lord of Ages wisely and patiently follows out the plan of His grace on behalf of us sinners. In recent times He has begun to bestow more generously upon divided Christians remorse over their divisions and a longing for unity" (**UR**, no.1).

As previously mentioned, this concern about Christian division surfaced in an evident way among Protestant missionaries and their churches at the beginning of the twentieth century. This gave rise in the 1920s to the "Faith and Order" and the "Life and Work" movements which sought to restore Christian unity. These movements coalesced in the 1940s to form the World Council of Churches.

The Catholic church, in the meantime, was pleased to see Protestant and Orthodox groups working out their divisions, but did not become involved in this effort. Catholic theology still insisted that the only authentic movement toward unity would be a return to the fullness of truth and Christian life found only in the Catholic church.

However, the Holy Spirit began to work a remarkable change in the Catholic church's attitude toward other Christians. In the mid-twentieth century, the Catholic church did not formally join other Christian movements or groups working toward unity, but did begin to send observers to their organizations. Also the efforts of a few individuals and small Catholic groups promoting Christian unity began to be heard and considered by recent popes.

This process culminated in the papacy of John XXIII, who

took some remarkable steps in promoting Christian unity. He invited delegates from the Protestant and Orthodox churches to observe the Second Vatican Council, and seated them in St. Peter's "front and center," directly across the aisle from the cardinals. He established a Secretariat for Promoting Christian Unity, giving it equal status to the other Council commissions. Thus Pope John XXIII accentuated the fact that the restoration of unity among Christians was among the primary goals of the Second Vatican Council.

Where does this issue stand today in the Catholic church? Is the pursuit of Christian unity still a top priority for Catholics? Has the ecumenical spirit become so much a part of the Catholic outlook and mentality that we can honestly say that "to be Catholic is to be ecumenical"? Officially, the Extraordinary Synod of Bishops in 1985 presented a positive and hopeful evaluation: "Basing itself on the ecclesiology of communion, the Catholic Church at the time of the Second Vatican Council fully assumed her ecumenical responsibility. After these twenty years we can affirm that ecumenism has inscribed itself deeply and indelibly in the consciousness of the Church" (**ES**, p.60).

There have been some great moments in ecumenism since the close of Vatican II: the lifting of the mutual excommunications of 1054 by Pope Paul VI and the Orthodox patriarch Athenagoras; historic meetings between the pope and the Archbishop of Canterbury; the establishment of official dialogues between the Catholic church and other Christian churches, and so on. But these efforts have also revealed how difficult and deep-rooted some of the issues and emotions are that divide us.

To be honest, the efforts of the Catholic church toward the restoration of Christian unity have barely begun. In many quarters, Catholics are not sufficiently informed about or interested in this topic. Unity among Christians sometimes bears greater resemblance to a secular indifferentism about matters of Christian faith than to an honest seeking of unity based upon the truth. For many people, to be "Christian" means little more than being loving and accepting, being a good person, or sharing common social concerns.

On the other hand, in some places we find a resurgence of the old hostilities and antagonisms among Christians being revived in the name of preserving Christian truth or "defending the faith." It is easy for Catholics to respond in kind to anti-Catholic sentiments and attitudes by launching our own truth crusade against others in a defensive spirit.

What is the Catholic challenge of ecumenism today? As we return to studying Vatican II's *Decree on Ecumenism* and sections of *The Dogmatic Constitution on the Church,* let us pray that the same Holy Spirit who stirred up this vision of Christian unity would rekindle this same vision and power today.

Catholics are now faced with the reality that Christian unity will not be attained and preserved by a short flurry of ecumenical enthusiasm, but will take many years of persistent study, commitment, dialogue, and prayer. We must be in it for the long haul, if God's purpose is to be accomplished. Catholics also must remain faithful to their church's teaching and norms for ecumenism if true unity is to be achieved. Let us examine, then, what direction the Second Vatican Council has provided concerning Christian unity.

What is ecumenism?

According to Vatican II's *Decree on Ecumenism,* ecumenism is "a movement, fostered by the grace of the Holy Spirit, for the restoration of unity among all Christians. Taking part in this movement are those who believe in the Triune God and confess Jesus as Lord and Savior" (no. 1).

Efforts for unity with non-Christians, which would include the Jewish people, are not properly part of the ecumenical movement. Also excluded from consideration here are groups that claim to be Christian but that do not believe in God as Trinity, nor in the divinity or "Lordship" of Jesus, such as the Mormons and the Jehovah's Witnesses.

It is important to note that the restoration of Christian unity is not to be achieved by human efforts alone, but from beginning to end it must be "fostered by the grace of the Holy Spirit."

Why strive to seek unity with other Christians?

Catholics have always believed that the church is one—that unity is an essential mark or characteristic of the true church of Christ. Hence, the Second Vatican Council proclaims that the restoration of unity among Christians is not optional. It is a gospel mandate. Jesus himself prayed fervently for the unity of his followers as being the will of his Father, and as a sign "that the world may believe that thou [the Father] hast sent me" (Jn 17:21).

The Holy Trinity itself is the model of the unity that Jesus' followers are to have with each other in the church (**UR**, no. 2). St. Paul taught that the church is "one body and one Spirit" (Eph 4:4ff.). He spent much of his ministry healing or preventing rifts, divisions, and factions among Christians for the sake of the unity of the body of Christ.

Christian unity is worth it because Jesus Christ wills it. He paid the price for unity, shedding his blood to form us into one people, one body—his people and his body on earth. As St. Paul exclaimed when he heard about disunity in the church at Corinth: "What, is Christ divided?!" Catholics must echo that same sentiment. "To be Catholic is to be ecumenical."

How should Catholics think about other Christians?

After the Protestant Reformation, it was common for Catholics and Protestants to think of each other as "heretics" (those who believed false doctrine), "schismatics" (those who divided the church), or "apostates" (those who renounced the true faith). This was also true of the relationship between Catholics and Orthodox Christians. These groups have had difficulty recognizing each other as true Christians.

What a radical departure from such a posture is the teaching of the Second Vatican Council! The Council proclaims, "All those justified by faith through baptism are incorporated into Christ. They therefore have a right to be honored by the title of Christian, and are properly regarded as brothers in the Lord by the sons of the Catholic Church" (**UR**, no. 2). Catholics look upon all those baptized into Christ and as our brothers and sisters in Christ, although they are "separated brethren," since "they do not profess the faith in its entirety or do not preserve unity of communion with the successor of Peter" (**LG**, no. 15).

Not only do Catholics recognize these baptized believers as Christians, but at Vatican II the Catholic church officially recognized for the first time the bodies to which these Christians belong as "churches and (ecclesial) communities." The Council recognized that the Spirit of Christ has used these churches as a means of salvation for their members.

Furthermore, *The Decree on Ecumenism* urges Catholics both to "joyfully acknowledge and esteem" the Christian elements in other churches, and even to learn from certain practices of other Christians, knowing that "whatever is wrought by the grace of the Holy Spirit in the hearts of our separated brethren can contribute to our own edification. Whatever is truly Christian never conflicts with the genuine interests of the faith; indeed it can always result in a more ample realization of the very mystery of Christ and the Church" (**UR,** no. 4).

How do Catholics now view the Orthodox churches?

Chapter 3 of *The Decree on Ecumenism* highlights the many common beliefs held by Catholics and the Eastern (Orthodox) Christians. The Eastern churches are of apostolic origin, and provide "a treasury from which the Church of the West has amply drawn for its liturgy, spiritual tradition, and jurisprudence" (no. 14). The first seven Ecumenical councils, recognized by both Eastern and Western Christianity, were held in the East.

The Second Vatican Council praises the Eastern churches' love of the sacred liturgy, especially the Eucharist, their devotion to Mary and the saints, their rich spiritual traditions, such as the Fathers of the church and monasticism, and their possession of true sacraments through apostolic succession.

Even those points of difference between the Catholic church and the Eastern churches, such as differences of theological expression, are seen by the Council as often complementary, rather than conflicting. For example, while Catholics speak of the life-giving presence of God in a person through the Holy Spirit as "sanctifying grace," the Orthodox speak of the "divine energies." The varying disciplines of the Eastern churches only add to the diverse beauty of the church.

In summary, the Second Vatican Council clearly indicates the great respect which the Catholic church has toward the Eastern Christian churches and their traditions. Catholics cherish the hope of attaining full unity with these churches, possibly in the near future. In seeking this unity, the Catholic church wishes to " 'impose no burden beyond what is indispensable' (Acts 15:28)" (**UR,** no. 18).

What about the differences between Catholics and Protestants?

The Decree on Ecumenism's perspective on the Protestant churches is noticeably different than its approach to the Orthodox Christian churches. While the common elements of belief among Catholics and Protestants are indeed listed, the Council alludes to "weighty differences" in understanding these elements and in the interpretation of revealed truth (no. 19).

These differences include the varying Catholic and Protestant understandings of the redemptive work of Christ, the role of Mary and the church in God's work of salvation (no. 20), the meaning of sacred Scripture and the relationship of Scripture to the church (no. 21), and the number and power of the sacraments (no. 22). Concerning the latter, the Council notes that Protestant churches "lack that fullness of unity with us which should flow from baptism and, . . . especially because of the lack of the sacrament of orders they have not preserved the genuine and total reality of the Eucharistic mystery. . . ." (no. 22).

It is necessary to be realistic about the unresolved differences that still divide Catholic and Protestant Christians. Nonetheless, the Council recognizes that our Protestant brethren are spiritually nourished by faith in Christ, baptism, hearing and meditating on God's Word in the Bible, private prayer, Christian family life, and community worship, which sometimes "displays notable features of an ancient, common liturgy" (no. 23).

What then is the goal of the ecumenical movement?

By definition, ecumenism seeks to bring Christians and their churches together in closer unity. Every step toward greater respect for other Christians and their traditions, working together in common mission and service while respecting doctrinal differences, and any progress toward agreement in doctrine advances the cause of Christian unity.

The final goal of ecumenism is expressed succinctly by the 1985 Extraordinary Synod, "We Bishops ardently desire that the incomplete communion already existing with the non-Catholic churches and communities might, with the grace of God, come to the point of full communion" (ES, p. 60).

Full communion would mean recognizing the same apostolic authority, professing the same essential Christian beliefs, and sharing fully in the same sacraments of the church. For Catholics, the climactic expression of full communion would be receiving the Eucharist together, after the necessary agreements about doctrine, worship, and common life had been reached. At that point, Christians could joyfully and sincerely join together as one to partake of the great sacrament of unity, the body and blood of the Lord in the Eucharist.

Until that day, Catholics must abstain from receiving communion in other Christian churches, save in exceptional circumstances. (In very limited and clearly defined circumstances, Catholics can receive the Eucharist in Christian churches which possess a valid sacrament of holy orders and believe as we do about the real presence of Christ in the Eucharist.)

Likewise, until full unity is achieved Christians of other churches are normally not permitted to receive Holy Communion in the Catholic church. For Catholics, receiving the Eucharist requires a belief in Jesus' real presence. This sacrament expresses the full unity of faith and life that we share with each other as Catholics and with the ordained apostolic ministers of the Catholic church. The Eucharist is a living sign of that deep unity and enriches that unity by the grace of Christ. We pray for the day when that depth of unity is established among all Christians, which is the goal of ecumenism.

Is renewal and repentance necessary for ecumenism?

It is imperative. *The Decree on Ecumenism* states that the "primary duty" of Catholics in ecumenical work is to honestly appraise what needs to be renewed and strengthened within the Catholic church. The Council calls all of us to repentance and reform. The decree states, "For although the Catholic Church has been endowed with all divinely revealed truth and with all means of grace, her members fail to live by them with all the fervor they should. As a result, the radiance of the Church's face shines less brightly in the eyes of our separated brethren and of the world at large, and the growth of God's kingdom is retarded. Every Catholic must therefore aim at Christian perfection... (cf. Jas 1:4; Rom 12:1-2)" (no. 4).

It is significant that rather than pointing the finger at the errors or faults of our separated brethren, the Council calls us to first reform and renew ourselves.

I have heard so many ex-Catholics say that they joined other churches because they were not being spiritually nourished in the Catholic church. Others say that they did not experience in their parish the fullness of Christian life that Catholic doctrine claims to possess. When the Catholic church lives out its doctrine fully and vibrantly, then Catholics will have no reason to leave. Then some of the greatest obstacles toward unity with other Christian churches and communities will be removed.

One of the mottos of the Catholic church must continue to be *Ecclesia semper reformanda:* "The church is always reforming herself." This is a prerequisite for successful ecumenism. "There can be no ecumenism worthy of the name without a change of heart. . . . Let all Christ's faithful remember that the more purely they strive to live according to the gospel, the more they are fostering and even practicing Christian unity. . . ." (no. 7).

What is the soul of the ecumenical movement?

The Decree on Ecumenism declares that "this change of heart and holiness of life, along with public and private prayer for the unity of Christians, should be regarded as the soul of the whole ecumenical movement, and can rightly be called 'spiritual ecumenism'" (no. 8).

The decree notes that Catholics already pray for Christian unity, and urges "that Catholics should join in prayer with their separated brethren" (no. 8), petitioning the Lord for the grace of unity. The annual Week of Prayer for Christian Unity in January is an important response to this call for prayer.

This teaching reminds Christians that unity is a gift from the Lord; and therefore, prayer for unity must be at the heart of all our ecumenical efforts.

Who is to initiate efforts for Christian unity?

After many years of peripheral involvement with the ecumenical movement, the Catholic church now realizes that if unity is God's will, Catholics must take a role of leadership. The Council states that, "Catholics must assuredly be concerned for their separated brethren, praying for them, keeping them informed about the Church, *making the first approaches towards them. . . .*" (no. 4, emphasis mine). Catholics are not to wait until we are approached, but are to take the initiative.

Is there a contradiction between ecumenism and leading other Christians to join the Catholic church?

The decree teaches that "the work of preparing and reconciling those individuals who wish for full Catholic communion is of its nature distinct from ecumenical action. But there is no opposition between the two, since both proceed from the wondrous providence of God" (no. 4).

This is certainly a sensitive area, but both activities are legitimate. If an individual hears God's call to join the Catholic church, the person must follow his or her leading of conscience, and the Catholic church should readily prepare and receive the person.

However, *The Decree on Ecumenism* reminds us that Christian unity will not be accomplished primarily by individuals changing churches. God's deepest desire is that Christian churches and ecclesial groups move together to restore the full unity of the one church of Jesus Christ. As all Christians focus on Jesus Christ and seek to conform their lives more fully to his teaching, Catholics believe that God will draw his people in all churches together into one.

What are some practical steps that we can take in seeking Christian unity?

The Decree on Ecumenism outlines some practical steps for ecumenical endeavors.

1. Catholics are to "eliminate words, judgments, and actions which do not respond to the condition of separated brethren with truth and fairness" (no. 4).
2. Catholics are to study the beliefs of other Christians in order to understand them correctly (no. 9).
3. Competent experts are to engage in ecumenical dialogue in order to know and appreciate the teaching and religious life of each communion, and possibly reach agreement in certain areas (nos. 4 and 9).
4. Christians of different churches can cooperate in projects and service for the common good (no. 4).
5. As mentioned above, Christians should come together for common prayer in ways that are permitted by their churches (no. 4).
6. After examining their own faithfulness to Christ's will for the church, all Christians should "undertake with vigor the task of renewal and reform" (no. 4).

7. Instruction in sacred theology, history, and other branches of knowledge must be presented from an ecumenical point of view.

This might appear theoretical, but any Catholic who has friends or acquaintances who belong to other Christian churches, or has simply struck up a conversation regarding Christianity with those of other traditions at social events or at ecumenical breakfasts or lunches, knows how useful and important these guidelines can be in building unity with these Christians.

These steps do foster unity. They should lead to closer communion among individual Christians and among the churches and ecclesial bodies to which they belong.

What are some pitfalls to ecumenism?

There appear to be two opposite dangers to true ecumenism that particularly affect Catholics. The *first* is an attitude that other Christian churches have nothing to offer us, since the Catholic church possesses the fullness of truth and the means of salvation. Catholics need to be reminded that there is no room for arrogance, pride, or "triumphalism" in approaching other Christians. Why? First, because we Catholics often fail to live the gospel as we should, despite the truth we possess and all the means of grace at our disposal. Humility is a more honest and Christian attitude.

In fact, *The Decree on Ecumenism* calls Catholics to repentance for our sins and failures. "St. John has testified: 'If we say that we have not sinned, we make him a liar, and his word is not in us' (1 Jn 1:10). This holds good for sins against unity. Thus, in humble prayer, we beg pardon of God and of our separated brethren, just as we forgive those who trespass against us" (no. 7).

The Decree on Ecumenism reminds Catholics that we can be instructed and edified by the lives and witness of other

Christians, which we will surely miss if we are so caught up in our own "fullness." One leading ecumenist warns of "Catholic sectarianism," (making Catholicism into a narrow sect), which happens when Catholics refuse to recognize the truly Christian elements in other Christian churches and ecclesial communities, pretending that we have no need of their witness of faith.

The *second danger* that threatens Catholic ecumenical efforts is a type of "religious indifferentism" or "non-denominationalism" that views different forms of Christianity as equally true and valid and that seeks unity based on a minimal doctrinal content upon which all Christians can agree. Perhaps you have heard people say things like, "All churches are pretty much the same," or "It doesn't matter what church you belong to or what you believe, as long as you are sincerely trying to be a Christian." (Often the term "good person" becomes interchangeable with the word "Christian.") This approach tends to downplay or overlook differences in belief. It focuses on the common elements of faith that are shared by most Christians.

While it is true that ecumenism is more fruitful when Christians *begin* by seeking and recognizing areas of agreement in faith and practice, true ecumenism cannot deny or overlook the differences and disagreements that divide Christians. *The Decree on Ecumenism* states that it is essential that doctrine be clearly presented in its entirety. Nothing is so foreign to the spirit of ecumenism as a *false conciliatory approach* [or "false irenicism"—Flannery ed.] which waters down or obscures the pure assured genuine meaning of Catholic doctrine (UR, no. 11).

"At the same time, Catholic belief needs to be explained more profoundly and precisely, in ways and in terminology which our separated brethren too can understand" (no. 11).

One of the greatest temptations in seeking unity is for Christians to water down or compromise their own doctrine in ecumenical dialogue, all for the sake of unity. Actually this is a disservice to the cause of unity, because doctrinal and other disagreements must be faced and honestly resolved. Unity must be based on truth.

Christians are genuinely united, even now, through love, the work of the Holy Spirit, and the beliefs and religious practices we hold in common. Yet Christians cannot settle for a fuller unity based upon a "least-common-denominator" Christianity that does not seek the fullness of Christian faith and life. We Catholics are not opposing ecumenism, therefore, when we speak in an open, honest way that is neither defensive nor aggressive about specifically Catholic doctrines (such as Catholic teaching about Mary, purgatory, or intercommunion). In doing this we are sharing aspects of our understanding of the fullness of Christian belief and life.

The Decree on Ecumenism does give a helpful hint to Catholics in speaking about their faith: "When comparing doctrine, they should remember that in Catholic teaching there exists an order or 'hierarchy' of truths, since they vary in their relationship to the foundation of the Christian faith" (no. 11). In other words, Catholics should distinguish between truths of the faith that are closer to the "heart" or foundation of Christianity, and those beliefs which we hold that are not as central to the basic gospel message (such as purgatory, indulgences, and devotions to particular saints). There is no official listing of this "hierarchy" of truths in order of importance or priority, but a sense of this may be gained through ongoing study of the sacred Scriptures and Catholic doctrine.

Catholics usually find that we agree with other Christians on most (if not all) of the primary elements of our faith, such as the incarnation, the resurrection, and the Second Coming. It is often the beliefs and practices that are less central to the heart of the gospel that divide us. However, we will still find disagreements with our separated brethren about what doctrines *are* most important and central to Christianity. Ecumenical dialogue seeks to reach agreement even concerning what is at the heart of Christian belief and practice, as well as discussing the specific beliefs that divide us.

Why shouldn't all Christians simply return to the Catholic church?

The Decree of Ecumenism does claim that "... it is through Christ's Catholic Church alone, which is the all-embracing means of salvation, that the fullness of the means of salvation can be obtained" (no. 3). In its doctrine, the Catholic church lacks nothing.

However, because of the division of Christianity, the Catholic church does not possess *in actuality* all of the essential marks of the true church of Christ in their perfect form. For example, since the one church has been divided, it is therefore no longer fully "catholic" or universal (no. 4). Elements of true apostolic succession exist outside the Catholic church, as well.

The conclusion to be drawn may sound contradictory: by Christ's gift, the Catholic church possesses the fullness of grace and the means of salvation; but because of the sin of division, the Catholic church is lacking in the actual expression of that fullness. Catholics must therefore join with other Christians in seeking the restoration of unity, so that the "one, holy, catholic and apostolic church" may be visibly present in the world in all its splendor and fullness.

Nowhere does Vatican II speak of ecumenism explicitly as a return to the Catholic church. Rather it speaks of Catholics joining with other Christians, focused on Jesus Christ, to seek the unity that God intends for his church. The result of this effort "will be that, little by little, as the obstacles to perfect ecclesiastical communion are overcome, all Christians will be gathered, in a common celebration of the Eucharist, into that unity of the one and only Church which Christ bestowed on His Church from the beginning" (no. 4).

Precisely how will this unity look? When and how will it

come about? The answer given is to be open to God's action and the inspiration of the Holy Spirit. The closing words of *The Decree on Ecumenism* remind Christians not to prejudge or obstruct the ways that God will use in the future to bring his church together into one. It also reminds us that this task is utterly beyond all human energies, ingenuity, and ability, and consequently the church "... places its hope entirely in the prayer of Christ for the Church, in the love of the Father for us, and in the power of the Holy Spirit. 'And hope does not disappoint, because the charity of God is poured forth in our hearts by the Holy Spirit who has been given to us' (Rom 5:5)" (no. 24).

The challenge of ecumenism continues to be one of the greatest challenges yet to be accepted and undertaken by most Catholics. The final chapter of the book will discuss two areas which are widely recognized as significant areas of concern and challenge for Catholics as well: education and the communications media.

RECOMMENDED READING

The Decree on Ecumenism (*Unitatis redintegratio*), Abbott ed., pp. 341-366; Flannery ed., pp. 452-470.

QUESTIONS FOR GROUP DISCUSSION

1. What is ecumenism? Why is it so important that it can be called the task of *every* Christian?

2. Why does ecumenism begin with our own repentance, reform, and renewal? Why is prayer for Christian unity called the "soul" of the ecumenical movement?

3. Are there any attitudes towards other Christians that you think need to change in order for you to view them as your brothers and sisters in Christ? What are some other practical ways that you could promote understanding and unity with other Christians? Discuss.

4. Why is it important in relating with other Christians to present fully and clearly what we believe as Catholics? Can we still learn from other Christians, even though we believe that the Catholic church possesses the fullness of Christian faith? Why?

5. What is the goal of the ecumenical movement? What do you think a fully united Christian church would look like? Discuss.

Personal Challenge

Ask yourself: Do I recognize that seeking Christian unity is one of my responsibilities and goals as a Catholic? What are my attitudes towards other Christians and their churches? Is there anything, such as a judgmental attitude, of which I need to repent? Am I willing to learn from and even be inspired by the lives of other Christians, both past and present? What can I do personally to promote unity with other Christians in my own life circumstances?

Practically speaking, what could I *really* do to express such unity? Have I considered joining with other Christians on some important moral or social issue of the day, such as pro-life work, caring for the homeless, or working for world peace and nuclear disarmament? Or perhaps I could consider praying with other Christians for unity on a regular basis, or join an ecumenical study group or Bible study that faithfully follows the norms of *The Decree on Ecumenism*?

Resource List

The lives or writings of great Christians of other churches, such as John Wesley's *Journal;* Protestant missionaries, such as Hudson Taylor; or others, such as the pioneer of Pentecostalism Smith Wigglesworth or the great Christian apologist C.S. Lewis.

Specifically, I can recommend:

The Life of Smith Wigglesworth, Jack Hywell-Davies (Ann Arbor, MI: Servant, 1988).

The Letters of C.S. Lewis and Don Giovanni Calabria: A Study in Friendship (Ann Arbor, MI: Servant, 1988). This book chronicles a correspondence of fifteen years between C.S. Lewis, an Anglican, and Fr. John Calabria, an Italian Roman Catholic priest.

For more serious study, one may read the documents of the international ecumenical dialogues between the Catholic church and other Christian churches. In particular, the Anglican-Roman Catholic International Commission of Theologians officially published on March 31, 1982, their *Final Report* on twelve years of dialogue, concerning subjects of belief and practice which have divided the two churches for more than four hundred years. The report is one of the first of its kind to elicit serious comment from the Vatican Congregation for the Doctrine of the Faith. To request information on this report or those generated by other ecumenical dialogues, write: The Graymoor Ecumenical Institute, 475 Riverside Drive, New York, New York 10115.

TEN

The Critical Challenges of the Media and Education

T HE DOCUMENTATION IS INCREASING every day about the tragic effects of pornography and violence in the media on the minds and lives of children and adults. Nearly every conceivable blasphemy and sin can be found graphically exhibited in movies and on television—not only in "adult" productions but even in "prime time" programming watched by millions of people of all ages. Even cartoons and other animated productions are not free of violent, occult, or other morally objectionable elements. Yet many parents still use the television as a "baby-sitter" without reviewing what their children watch. The same type of problem exists in the media of music, periodicals, "comic books," and news-papers.

These media have become some of the most powerful educational tools in our time. As with nearly every facet of modern life, they can be of great benefit when used to present good morality, sound education, helpful informa-tion, wholesome entertainment, and even the truths of religion. But they can be of great danger and harm when their use becomes disengaged from the moral order and from those things which contribute to authentic, full human life as God intended it.

Adults, especially parents, become the key figures today in determining what sort of media exposure and education they will allow and choose for themselves and for their children. We must first decide what to read, watch, and listen to in order to promote our own growth. We must decide how we will respond to media or educational institutions when they present things we judge to be good (Will we support them?) or evil (Will we speak out against them?). Parents must take responsibility for what their children see and hear and for how they are educated. They need to help their children discern for themselves what is true and worthwhile and what is not. Parents must take seriously their own role as educators, especially with regard to faith. It is irresponsible to simply leave this to others, regardless of how qualified teachers may be.

A couple of years ago, my son attended a Catholic school which provided excellent religious instruction. We often took advantage of this to discuss at meals some of the things he had been learning about the faith. Recently I began the custom of spending a half hour to an hour on Sunday with my children studying a catechism, reading and discussing Scripture, or going over parts of the Mass and discussing how we participate. No matter how good the religious education may be in a school or a CCD program, children must experience their home as a primary place for prayer and instruction—as a place where their Catholic faith is lived out daily.

Since there are few things which shape and form the human person and society today as decisively as educational institutions and the communications media, the Fathers of the Second Vatican Council decided to devote separate documents to each of these topics. They wisely saw that these subjects each merited their own document, rather than devoting only a single chapter or section to them in the constitution on the church or the constitution on the church in the modern world.

Even so, these two documents of Vatican II have both been criticized by some because of their brevity and allegedly superficial analysis. The documents follow the pattern of laying out general principles and suggestions, leaving the development of more specific and in-depth strategies to the labor of others.

It has been argued that the Catholic bishops do not speak as professional educators nor as experts in the mass media. Generally, they are not, but in these documents they speak with competence as the church's shepherds, commenting on the pastoral implications of these forces upon the faith and life of God's people. The church itself is an educator and a communicator, and has a deserved interest and concern for how all education and the mass media affect society.

Let us look at each document to discover the principles and guidelines they present.

What is the purpose of education?

The Declaration on Christian Education (**GE**, *Gravissinum educationis*) states, "A true education aims at the formation of the human person with respect to his ultimate goal" (no. 1), and with respect to the good of society. Therefore, not only does each person have "an inalienable right to an education corresponding to his proper destiny" (no. 1), but each Christian "is entitled to a Christian education" (no. 2).

Besides developing a person's physical, moral, and intellectual endowments, a Christian education: 1. introduces a person into a knowledge of the mystery of salvation, based on the gift of faith; 2. teaches a person to adore God in spirit and truth (Jn 4:23), especially through liturgical worship;

3. trains the person to conduct his or her personal life in righteousness and truth, modeled after Christ himself (Eph 4:13, 22-24); 4. helps the person grow accustomed to giving witness to the faith and hope that is in him or her (1 Pt 3:15), and to promoting the Christian transformation of the world (no. 2).

Whose obligation is education?

Parents are the "first and foremost educators of their children." The Christian education document stresses that their role as educators is so decisive that scarcely anything else can compensate for their failure in it. It is the parents' responsibility to create a family atmosphere "animated with love and reverence for God and men." The goal is that the children will grow in virtue and become well-rounded in personal and social skills (no. 3). In the family, children first learn to know and worship God, to love their neighbor and experience human companionship, and to belong to the church and society.

Society as a whole must assist in the work of education by supporting "the rights of parents and of others to whom parents entrust a share in the work of education" (no. 3). This support is part of society's responsibility to promote the common good. Note that society is not given the task of being the primary educator, but the state is to assist the parents and those whom the parents authorize to teach their children. In the United States, it often appears that the government has established itself as primary educator. It is the parents who must conform to the dictates, wishes, and guidelines of the state. This is *not* the Catholic church's perspective!

The church educates by announcing and teaching the way of salvation in Jesus Christ, especially through the liturgy and catechetical instruction (no. 4). The church also promotes and supports the full human development of each person for his or her own welfare and that of society. Let us discuss now the place of schools in this scheme.

What is the church's position concerning schools?

Schools are viewed as particularly valuable agencies of education. The vocation of a school teacher is praised as "beautiful" and "truly solemn" (no. 5). Parents should be free in their choice of schools, even from the standpoint of economics. The document calls for the allocation of public subsidies to enable parents to send their children to the schools of their choice (no. 6).

The declaration warns against any attempt of the state to monopolize the entire educational system. The faithful are urged to get involved with the teachers and the school system, such as through parents' associations.

Finally, the church must recognize her "very grave obligation to give zealous attention to the moral and religious education of all her children," and to offer special services and programs, such as CCD, for those not in Catholic schools. The goal here is that children "pace their development as Christians with their growth as citizens of the world" (no. 7).

What about Catholic schools?

The Catholic school is recommended to all Catholic parents, since it can create "an atmosphere enlivened by the gospel spirit of freedom and charity" (no. 8). The Catholic school aims to match spiritual development with human and cultural development.

Despite changing times, this declaration asserts the "immense importance" of Catholic schools and asserts "the Church's right freely to establish and run schools of every kind and at every level" (no. 8). It is a sad irony that in some countries, such as the United States, thousands of Catholic schools have closed since the Second Vatican Council due to lack of financial support and decline in dedicated religious and priests available to teach in the schools, as well as other factors. Even now the future of Catholic schools in many countries remains uncertain. Today Catholics face many challenges with regard to Catholic education, including how to provide suitable Catholic education for their children when the Catholic schools have closed; how to maintain a strong Christian orientation for existing Catholic schools; and how to keep tuition for Catholic schools moderate enough so that the poor and even middle class Catholics are not excluded.

The declaration emphasizes the importance of good teachers in the success of the Catholic school. It urges that they be certified, trained with care in both secular and religious knowledge, and have up-to-date educational skill. Most importantly, "bound by charity to one another and to their students, and penetrated by an apostolic spirit, let them give witness to Christ, the unique Teacher, by their lives as well as by their teachings. Above all, let them perform their services as partners of the parents. . . ." (no. 8).

Catholic schools must deal with specific issues in a Christian way, such as recognition of the importance of sexual differences. The Council states, "they should pay due regard in every educational activity to sexual differences and to the special role which divine Providence allots to each sex in family life and in society" (no. 8).

In responding to the demands of modern conditions, the declaration recommends the founding of professional and technical schools, institutes for adult education, social services, schools for students with special needs, schools for preparing Catholic teachers, and so on. Whatever the school or program attended, "The purpose in view is that by living an exemplary and apostolic life, the Catholic graduate can become, as it were, the saving leaven of the human family" (no. 8).

What about Catholic institutions of higher learning?

The Declaration on Christian Education affirms the church's support of schools of higher learning, especially colleges and universities. The declaration advocates the pursuit of truth "with the freedom of scientific investigation," while believing that "faith and reason give harmonious witness to the unity of all truth," as St. Thomas Aquinas and all the church's most illustrious teachers have taught.

No one could have ever guessed the traumatic changes that have occurred in these Catholic institutions, at least in the West, since the close of the Second Vatican Council.

Today many Catholic colleges and universities are declaring their independence from the *magisterium* of the Catholic church, as if faith and reason were at odds. How un-Catholic! The fear that the church's teaching office may stifle free academic inquiry is a current concern among some Catholics, but it certainly finds no basis in this declaration. This declaration assumes that the *magisterium* of the Catholic church has the right to teach the Catholic faith authoritatively. Those who teach in a Catholic university should certainly be expected to respect this authoritative teaching role of the *magisterium* and not advocate views that contradict Catholic teaching.

Recent popes such as John Paul II have also tried to clarify this issue. In session with some U.S. bishops in Rome on Oct. 15, 1988, Pope John Paul II explained that faith does not limit freedom in the pursuit of knowledge. Faith does not stifle the inquiries of reason or science, which are properly governed by their own principles and methodologies. Rather, faith assists reason in achieving the full good of the human person and society by recognizing the transcendent dimension of the human person. Faith preserves the full truth about humanity; "for this reason the university by its nature is called to be ever more open to the senses of the absolute and the transcendent, in order to facilitate the search for truth at the service of humanity."[1]

Besides advancing the quest for knowledge in consonance with the fundamental truths about humanity's nature and true good, the Catholic university also can assist in the "re-evaluation" of society that Pope John Paul II has called for. In order to engage in this, Catholics must know their faith. The Pope speaks of the *right* of Catholic university students to receive a Catholic formation, both doctrinal and moral, that corresponds to the level of their scholastic abilities. It is obvious that if Catholic students hope to have an impact on higher culture and witness to their faith before the world, they must be clear about their own Catholic identity, and so must the colleges and universities in which they are formed. The pope insists, "This Catholic identity has to be present in the fundamental direction given to both teaching and studies."[2]

Returning to the Council's *Declaration on Catholic Education*, Catholic institutions should be located around the world and distinguished for their academic pursuits rather than the size of their enrollment. They should open their doors to students of special promise "even though of slender means, especially those who come from young [developing] nations" (no. 10). The church should also establish residences and outreaches to support the spiritual life of Catholics and other students at colleges and universities which are not Catholic (no. 10).

What are we to make of the freedom of Catholic theologians?

Since theology deals with the exposition of truth as seen through the light of faith, it is overseen by the bishops of the church who have been given special authority by Christ to discern and teach matters of faith. (This authority is discussed regarding the interpretation of Scripture in *The Constitution on Divine Revelation*, article 12, and in *The Dogmatic*

Constitution on the Church, articles 23 and 25.)

All of the Vatican II documents encourage advanced scholarship, including scientific research, even in theology. In an age marked by competition between different fields of study and among schools, the call for cooperation among Catholic scholars and schools is refreshingly significant. A broad range of theological inquiry may be carried on within the wide boundaries of theological orthodoxy set by the church's teaching office over the centuries.

Yet considerable tension still exists between some theologians and the *magisterium* of the church, which the Extraordinary Synod of 1985 recommends as a priority to resolve. (See **ES**, p. 51, the section concerning "the relationship between the magisterium of the Bishops and theologians.") Recently the Sacred Congregation for the Doctrine of the Faith in Rome took a major step in clarifying the proper relationship between theologians and the official teachers (*magisterium*) of the church by publishing a document, *Instruction On the Ecclesial Vocation of the Theologian.*[3] Through study and discussion of this document, Catholics may confidently hope that the theologian's role in the church and in the formation of our faith may be better understood.

What is the purpose of ecclesiastical universities and faculties of sacred science?

Section 2 of *The Declaration on Christian Education* underscores the importance of these faculties which prepare students for the priesthood and advanced chairs of teaching and research. These faculties seek to develop the deeper understanding of sacred revelation, unfold the treasures of Christian wisdom in the church, and foster dialogue with our separated brethren and with non-Christians (no. 11).

In April of 1979, Pope John Paul II issued an important apostolic constitution, *On Christian Wisdom (Sapientia*

Christiana)[4], giving specific guidelines for ecclesiastical universities and faculties.

What are the prospects for Catholic education?

The conclusion of this document focuses on the debt of gratitude that Catholics owe to "those priests, religious men and women, and lay people who in their evangelical self-dedication devote themselves to the surpassing work of education." Young people are "urgently" implored to consider teaching as a vocation (no. 12).

The future of Catholic education does hinge largely on Catholic *teachers*. Will there continue to be enough priests and religious men and women involved in education to support even a steadily declining number of Catholic schools? Will lay people be paid enough to make teaching in a Catholic school a realistic option, especially those married and desiring to raise families according to the church's own teaching? At present, we may *say* that Catholic teachers are important, but we *pay* them as if they were among the least important. Even more critically, where will Catholic teachers be instructed in the authentic and full teaching of the Catholic faith, without confusion or compromise, so they will be able to hand on a living faith to their students?

The future of Catholic education also hinges on Catholic *schools*. Will they preserve their authentic *Catholic identity*, and thus be able to influence both their students and the broader society by means of the truths and values of the kingdom of God? As Pope John Paul II has said, "The adjective 'Catholic' must always be the real expression of a profound reality."[5] Schools that are Catholic in name only are useless to God and to his people. Eventually they will die or become thoroughly secularized, indistinguishable from their secular counterparts.

The Catholic challenge in education is to support and

promote all forms of education that are academically sound and genuinely Catholic in every respect.

What forms of media are discussed in this document?

The Decree on the Instruments of Social Communication (**IM,** *Inter mirifica*) is one of the shortest documents of the Council and one of the first two to be passed, along with *The Constitution on Sacred Liturgy.*

Why? Because of the ever-increasing influence on society of the contemporary media (as I described in opening this chapter), the church's teaching on the proper use of the mass media becomes ever more crucial. Although this decree spells out only the first, rudimentary principles to be considered, certainly if these basic principles had been taught and followed, the media and society today would be significantly improved, at least in the West. Let us test this hypothesis by outlining the teaching of this decree and ask whether it has been heard and followed.

Included in this discussion are means of communication which by their very nature can reach and influence the whole of society: the press, movie theatres, radio, television, and similar media. The church, as a mother, naturally is concerned about the influence they have on her children:

Mother Church, to be sure, recognizes that if these instruments are rightly used they bring solid nourishment to the human race. For they can contribute generously to the refreshment and refinement of the spirit, and to the spread and strengthening of God's own kingdom.

But the Church is also aware that men can employ these gifts against the mind of the divine Benefactor, and abuse them to their own undoing. In fact, the Church grieves with a motherly sorrow at the damage far too often inflicted on society by the perverse use of these media. (no. 2)

What should the church's goals be with regard to the mass media?

This decree specifies two goals: first, to *use* the instruments of social communication to proclaim to the world the good news of redemption in Jesus Christ; second, to *instruct* humanity in the worthy use of these instruments, and to animate their use "with a humane and Christian Spirit" (no. 3).

But how can we insure the media are used properly?

The first necessary step is that all who use the media know the norms of morality and apply them faithfully. Catholics must be educated to recognize what is moral and what is immoral through the study of the sacred Scripture and the church's teaching and tradition. Catholics must examine the moral quality of the subject matter, as well as the "context" (such as intention, audience, place, and time) which can modify [the media's] moral quality or even reverse it entirely (no. 4).

An evident example is that some TV productions, which may be unobjectionable for adults, such as a graphic documentary portraying warfare, might be harmful for children. Therefore, they should not be aired when or where children would be a large part of the audience. The Council notes that some instruments of the media are so powerful and compelling "that people, especially if they are caught off guard, may scarcely be able to appreciate it, to moderate it, or, when necessary, to reject it" (no. 4). An extreme case of this would be subliminal or subaudial messages of which the person is not even aware. A more frequent situation involves people in public transportation or other public facilities where constant music and a barrage of commercial messages are practically impossible for people to "tune out" or ignore.

What are some key areas for taking a stand morally?

This decree gives three specific examples in which an upright conscience will desire to follow moral norms: First, the *"right to information."* People do have the right to know about affairs which affect them individually and collectively. The moral standards involved here insist that information "always be true and complete as charity and justice allow." Further, "in the gathering and publication of news . . . the legitimate rights and dignity of a man must be held sacred" (no. 5). In other words, the right to information does not mean that anyone has a right to know about another person's private affairs, unless they pose some threat to the common good. Also information cannot be obtained by morally illicit means.

Second, *concerning art.* Sometimes we hear of the presentation of material in the media justified as "art" which is of questionable moral content—even something as abominable and degrading to persons as pornography. The Council warns against "ethical and artistic theories which are false." It "asserts that the primacy of the objective moral order demands absolute allegiance" (no. 6). Only the moral order established by God proposes and judges the true value of all human endeavors, including art.

Third, *portrayal of moral evil.* There is some justification for the portrayal of moral evil by the media, nonetheless "moral norms must prevail if harm rather than spiritual profit is not to ensue. This requirement is especially needed when subjects treated are entitled to reverence, or may all too easily trigger base desires in man, wounded as he is by original sin" (no. 7). A good example of this has been the tendency since the late 1970s by Hollywood to produce

movies that glorify anti-heroes—men and women who lack
any authentic morality and have no recognizable redeeming
vitues.

Who has moral responsibility for proper use of the media?

This is the heart of *The Decree on the Instruments of Social
Communication.* Moral responsibility for the proper use of the
media fall primarily upon three groups: 1.) the "consumers
or users of the media; 2.) the "makers" and transmitters of
the media; and 3.) the civil authorities. Each of these are
discussed in detail.

What is the moral responsibility of the consumers?

The first and primary responsibility for the correct use of
the media falls on "those readers, viewers, or listeners who
personally and freely choose to receive what these media
have to communicate" (no. 9). It may appear obvious, but
the easiest way to avoid moral evil in the media, or even
presentations of questionable value, is to turn off the TV set
or radio, or put down the offending book or magazine. The
Council instructs that in our selection of media we should
amply favor "whatever fosters virtue, knowledge, or art.
People should reject whatever could become a cause or an
occasion of spiritual harm to themselves, whatever could
endanger others through bad example, and whatever would
impede good selections and promote bad ones" (no. 9).

Consumers of the media must *learn* to make good judgments and to form their consciences according to the moral
law by listening to competent authorities. This process must
begin in youth. Just think how much the following advice
has been *needed* over the past twenty-five years, especially
with the use of TV and radio. Yet how little it has been *heeded.*
"People, especially the young, should take care to develop
moderation and self-control in the use of these instruments.
Their goal should be an ever more discerning grasp of what

they see, hear, and read. Discussions with educators and appropriate experts will school them to make mature judgments" (no. 10).

Even more critical is the following instruction to *parents:* "Parents should be mindful of their duty to guard against shows, publications, and the like which would jeopardize faith or good morals. *Let them see that such things never cross the thresholds of their homes and that their children do not encounter them elsewhere"* (no. 10, emphasis mine).

Would a parent readily invite a drug pusher, a punk rock star, someone sexually perverted, or a user of foul language into his or her home to sit down with the children and instruct them? And yet it happens every day in modern homes where such media figures are viewed as "baby-sitters" and entertainers of youth. Catholics must assume *primary moral responsibility* for what comes into their homes, and into their own minds and the minds of those whom they raise or pastor.

What is the moral responsibility of the "makers"?

The church says that the "chief moral duties" for the proper use of the media fall on "newsmen, writers, actors, designers, producers, exhibitors, distributors, operators, and sellers, critics, and whoever else may have a part of any kind in making and transmitting products of communication." Through their activity, they can lead the human race "upward or to ruin" (no. 11).

Is this an exaggeration? When you consider the influence of the media—no. The Council demands that the producers of the media regulate their own activity according to moral standards and pursuit of the common good, and not merely according to the amount of profit they can make. "These responsible persons should never forget that much of their audience consists of young people who have need of literature and shows that can give them decent amusement and inspiration" (no. 11). Jesus said something about millstones around the necks of those who led the "little ones" astray (Mt 18:6; Mk 9:42; Lk 17:2).

What moral responsibility do civil authorities have?

The mass media are subordinate to the common good, which civil authority is pledged to uphold. Civil authority must insure the availability of true information, and should "foster religion, culture, and fine arts" (no. 12).

Public authority also has a *protective* role, which is to ensure "that serious danger to public moral and social progress do not result from a perverted use of these instruments." Civil authorities have a right and a duty to pass laws that protect public morality and the dignity of persons, and to energetically enforce these laws. This watchfulness on behalf of the common good is not an infringement of individual rights any more than are laws against robbery, assault, or murder. These laws are justified especially if those who have taken upon themselves the responsibility of using these media have failed to respect the common good and the rights and dignity of each person.

The decree again stresses that "Particular effort should be expended to protect youngsters from literature and shows which would be injurious to them at their age" (no. 12).

In summary, when the consumers of the media are not discriminating nor willing to speak out and the makers and transmitters of the media are irresponsible in what they produce and transmit, then the civil authority is the last line of protection against the misuse of media. Realistically, such pervasive misuse could destroy a nation from within—by destroying its moral fiber and commitment to promoting the good of all.

What should the church do?

The church should be the most effective and influential moral force behind the proper and constructive use of the mass media. The decree encourages pastors to use the media to spread the gospel and urges Christian lay persons involved with their use to "be busy giving witness to Christ, especially by performing their duties skillfully and with apostolic ardor" (no. 13).

Catholics are to provide leadership in the media: by establishing "a Catholic press worthy of the name" and encouraging good moral values by "the production and showing of films which serve honest relaxation as well as culture and art"; by patronage of "theatres managed by upright Catholics and others"; by supporting decent radio and television productions, "particularly those which are proper family fare"; and even by making efforts "to establish Catholic stations" that "excel in professional quality and forcefulness" (no. 14).

In the United States, who has done more for Catholic television than Mother Angelica, whose apostolic zeal led to the foundation of a nationwide Catholic cable television network of excellent professional quality and sound religious and family programming? The decree comments that "It would be dishonorable indeed if sons of the Church sluggishly allowed the word of salvation to be silenced or impeded by the technical difficulties or the admittedly enormous expenses which are characteristic of these instruments" (no. 17). Mother Angelica's witness proves that nothing is impossible, technically or financially, to those who have faith and seek only to do God's will.

The question is whether Catholics will heed the Council's challenge to support and assist Catholic newspapers, magazines, movie enterprises, and radio and television stations and programs "whose main purpose is to spread and defend the truth and to strengthen the Christian texture of human society" (no. 17).

In order for Catholic media leadership to grow, priests, religious, and laity must be trained to carry out this task through schools and institutes where they can obtain up-to-date, well-rounded formation animated by a Christian spirit (no. 15).

The decree recommends that the bishops of the church plan a media apostolate (no. 21) and oversee and promote proper use of the media in their dioceses (no. 20). Bishops are further advised to "devote a day of each year to instructing the faithful in their duties on this subject," so that the faithful might pray for the media and support those Catholic institutes and enterprises meeting the needs of the world in this field (no. 18). In fact, the United States bishops have worked together toward this end.

The decree rightly observes in its concluding statement, "The fate of humanity grows daily more dependent on the right use of these media" (no. 24). To take up this challenge, Catholics need further instruction and reflection on this vast and important area.[6]

Can Catholics win, or win back, the educational establishment and the media fully to Christ and his church? Only time will tell. But, prayerfully and soberly, each of us needs to begin doing our own part in meeting these immense challenges.

RECOMMENDED READING

Declaration on Christian Education (*Gravissimum educationis*), Abbott ed., pp. 637-651; Flannery ed. pp. 725-737.

Decree on the Instruments of Social Communication (*Inter mirifica*), Abbott ed., pp. 319-331; Flannery ed., pp. 283-292.

QUESTIONS FOR GROUP DISCUSSION

1. What is distinctive about the Catholic view of the goals of education?

2. How do Catholics view the role and responsibilities of *parents* in the education of youth? of *teachers*? of *society*? of the *church*? Discuss.

3. What does the declaration on education say about the value and importance of Catholic schools? What is the distinctive purpose of such schools, including colleges and universities?

4. Why does the decree on the media emphasize that people must know and obey objective standards of morality in the production and use of TV, radio, movies, and other media?

5. What are the responsibilities of the *users* of the media? of the *writers or producers*? of the *government*? Discuss.

6. What challenge does this decree present to the church in particular?

7. Has the Catholic church been successful in carrying out the Council's teaching on education and the media? Explain.

PERSONAL CHALLENGE

How have I contributed to Catholic education? Do I see the church's mission of education as valuable and worthy of my personal support? If I am a parent, do I take seriously my responsibilities as the primary educator of my children? If I am a teacher, do I take seriously the important vocation God has given me? Do I see areas of improvement needed in the Catholic mission of education? How could I contribute to this improvement?

Do the "media" seem to be promoting moral values that are objectively true and upbuilding to my life and that of society? If not, what could I do to influence the media and help them promote positive human and Christian values? Do I monitor my own exposure to the media, and those of my family and others whom I care for, so that media exposure is a positive influence? How could I support Catholic efforts in the media, which promote positive human and Christian values and present the teaching of the church fully and accurately?

RESOURCE LIST

*On Catechesis in Our Time, **Catechesi Tradendae**,* Pope John Paul II, October 16, 1979.

*Pastoral Instruction on the Means of Social Communication (**Communio et Progressio**),* January 29, 1971, found in Vatican II documents, Flannery ed., pp. 293-349.

Conclusion

Vatican II: The Catholic Challenge is a tool that can be used in the spiritual development in the life of every sincere and dedicated Catholic Christian today. It calls each of us to the fullness of our identity in every aspect of our lives.

We are the people gifted with God's Word, who are challenged to know and live that Word as it comes to us in sacred Scripture, sacred Tradition, and through the teaching office of the pope and the bishops.

We are the people whose worship of God as a community in the liturgy is the fullest expression of who we are and the summit of our life. Thus we are challenged to worship our Lord reverently and faithfully, in spirit and truth.

We are the people of God, whose fullness resides in the Catholic church. Yet we recognize the gifts and grace of God at work in other baptized believers.

We are the people of God who have different gifts, callings, and positions of service in the body of Christ. Yet all are equally called to holiness and Christian perfection. All of us must accept Christ's challenging call to be saints.

We are the missionary people of God called by Christ to spread the good news through the world and to make disciples of all nations—including those closest to us, those with whom we live, work, and recreate. At the same time, we must respect each individual's right to believe as his or her conscience dictates. We must also respect what is good and true in other religions, as we present to them the truth found in Jesus Christ and his teaching.

We are the people of God, called to work with charity and understanding toward the unity of al Christians, even as we remain firmly committed to the fullness of our own Catholic faith.

We are the people of God challenged to take up the mission of Christ in every sphere of human life: the family, politics, economics, social and cultural life, educations, and the mass media. Our aim is that Christ may truly be the Lord of all, in every aspect of life.

Relying on God's grace and guidance, we trust that this Catholic challenge is only the beginning of a new endeavor among Catholic Christians: to live and proclaim the gospel of Jesus Christ with new boldness and understanding at the dawn of the third millennium.

Notes

Introduction

1. *Catholicism and Modernity*, (New York: Seabury, 1979), p. 223.
2. Pope John XXIII, "Pope John's Opening Speech to the Council," October 11, 1962 in *The Documents of Vatican II*, Walter Abbott, S.J., ed., (Piscataway, NJ: America Press/New Century, 1966), pp. 710-719.

ONE
Knowing and Living God's Word

1. *The Ratzinger Report*, (San Francisco: Ignatius Press, 1985), p. 76.

TWO
The Church: A Mystery and the People of God

1. See Francis Sullivan, S.J., "The Significance of the Vatican II Declaration that the Church of Christ 'Subsists in' the Roman Catholic Church," in *Vatican II: Assessment and Perspectives*, Vol. II, ed. by Rene Latourelle (New York: Paulist, 1989), pp. 272-287.
2. See Michael Schmaus, *Dogma 4: The Church*, p. 209.
3. John Paul II, *Vicesimus Quintus*, "On the 25th Anniversary of the Constitution on the Sacred Liturgy," December 4, 1988. *The Pope Speaks*, Sept./Oct., 1988, p. 225.

THREE
Touching Eternity: The Call to Worship

1. Pope John Paul II. *Vicesimus quintus*, "On the 25th Anniversary of the Constitution on the Sacred Liturgy," *The Pope Speaks*,

Sept./Oct., 1989, p. 231. Henceforth, **VQ** in parentheses in the text.

2. *On the Mystery and Worship of the Eucharist,* (***Dominicae Cenae***), 13, February 24, 1980.

SEVEN
The Challenge to Bishops, Priests, and Religious

1. Also see "Women Priests: Why Not?," Msgr. Desmond Connell, *L'Osservatore Romano,* English Ed., March 7, 1988, pp. 6-8, 10.

EIGHT
Proclaiming the Gospel

1. It is instructive to compare the official Catholic liturgical prayers for the Jewish people in the Good Friday liturgy as they have been revised according to this teaching of Vatican II. In the Roman Missal of Pope Pius V, used until 1966, Catholics prayed, "Let us pray for the perfidious (faithless) Jews; that Our God and Lord would withdraw the veil from their hearts; that they also may acknowledge Our Lord Jesus Christ."

    In the re-used Roman Missal of 1966, Catholics prayed, "Let us also pray that Our God and Lord will look kindly on the Jews; so that they too may acknowledge the Redeemer of all, Jesus Christ, Our Lord."

    Finally, in the Roman Missal of 1975 in current use, we pray, "Let us pray for the Jewish people, the first to hear the word of God, that they may continue to grow in the love of His name and in faithfulness to His covenant."

2. Peter Kreeft, *Fundamentals of Christian Faith,* (San Francisco: Ignatius, 1988), p. 142.

TEN
The Critical Challenge of the Media and Education

1. "The universal ordinary magisterium can be considered to be the usual expression of the Church's infallibility," Pope John Paul II, *L'Osservatore Romano,* English ed., Oct. 24, 1988, p. 22.
2. Ibid.

3. *L'Osservatore Romano,* Eng. ed., July 2, 1990, pp. 1-4; *Origins,* Vol. 20, No. 8, July 5, 1990, pp. 117, 119-126.

4. *Apostolic Constitution on Ecclesiastical Universities and Faculties (Sapientia Christiana),* Pope John Paul II, April 29, 1979.

5. Address to Bishops of U.S.A. on *Ad Limina* visit, in *L'Osservatore Romano,* Oct. 24, 1988, p. 22.

6. One post-conciliar document which complements and completes this decree of the Second Vatican Council is the *Pastoral Instruction on the Means of Social Communication, Communio et Progressio,* January 27, 1971, which is published in the 1981 Austin Flannery edition of *Vatican II: The Conciliar and Post Conciliar Documents* (Grand Rapids, MI: Eerdmans, 1981).

Other Books to Strengthen Your Catholic Faith by Alan Schreck

Catholic and Christian

A readable and concise explanation of commonly misunderstood Catholic beliefs—the teachings and practices that don't get much attention in Sunday homilies but which puzzle Catholics and other Christians alike. A book for all Catholics who want to understand their faith better. *$8.99*

Basics of the Faith: A Catholic Catechism

A masterful catechism designed to lead readers to a deeper appreciation and understanding of Catholic Christianity. An up-to-date and reliable guide, presented in a way that modern readers can appreciate—clearly setting forth the teachings of the church in an age characterized by moral and religious relativism. *$9.99*

The Compact History of the Catholic Church

A lively and readable history. Designed as an introduction to Catholicism, this convenient resource offers more than just names, dates, and places. Dr. Schreck covers not only the topics and issues of each period but also skillfully guides us through the maze of politics, scandals, and heresies that have challenged the church both from within and without. *$7.99*